More STORIES OF
Dogs
AND THE
LIVES THEY TOUCH

More Stories of Dogs and the Lives They Touch

AND THE Lives They Touch

Edited by Peggy Schaefer

Ideals Publications
Nashville, Tennessee

ISBN 0-8249-4639-1

Published by Ideals Publications, a division of Guideposts
535 Metroplex Drive, Suite 250, Nashville, Tennessee 37211
www.idealsbooks.com

Copyright © 2005 by Ideals Publications

Printed and bound in the U.S.A. by RR Donnelley

Library of Congress Cataloging-in-Publication Data
More stories of dogs and the lives they touch / edited by Peggy Schaefer.
     p. cm.
  ISBN 0-8249-4639-1 (alk. paper)
  1. Dogs—Anecdotes. 2. Dog owners—Anecdotes. 3. Human-animal
relationships—Anecdotes. I. Schaefer, Peggy, date.
  SF426.2.M66 2005
  636.7—dc22

                              2004023616

Publisher, Patricia A. Pingry   Assistant Editor, Melinda Rathjen
Associate Publisher, Peggy Schaefer   Copy Editors, Marie Brown,
Series Designer, Marisa Calvin   Melinda Rathjen

Front jacket photo © Rachael Hale Photography Limited 2005. All rights reserved.
Rachael Hale is a registered trade mark of Rachael Hale Photography Limited.

10 9 8 7 6 5 4 3 2 1

ACKNOWLEDGMENTS

ALAN, JACK. An excerpt from *How to Raise a Dog*. Copyright © 1944 by Jack Goodman and Alan Green.
Published by Simon & Schuster. ALBRECHT, KATHY ELLEN with Jana Murphy. "One Red Hound" from *The
Lost Pet Chronicles*. Copyright © by the authors. Published by Bloomsbury Publishers, NY. KNAPP, CAROLINE.
"Fantasy Dog" from *Pack of Two*. Copyright © 1998 by Caroline Knapp. Used by permission of The Dial
Press/Dell Publishing, a division of Random House, Inc. LINGENFELTER, MICHAEL and David Frei. "Dakota's
Gift" from *The Angel By My Side*. Copyright © 2002 by the authors. Reprinted by permission of Michael
Lingenfelter. PATCHETT, ANN. "This Dog's Life" from *Dog is my Co-Pilot*. Compiled by the editors of *The Bark*.
Copyright © 2003. SIGMAN, ELENA. Adapted from "The Existence of Dog" © 2002 by Elena Sigman, which
originally appeared on Salon.com and was reprinted in *Dog Is My Co-Pilot*, compiled by the Editors of *The
Bark*, Crown Pub., © 2003. STEINBECK, JOHN. An excerpt from *Travels With Charley* by John Steinbeck.
Copyright © 1961, 1962 by The Curtis Publishing Co., © 1962 by John Steinbeck, renewed © 1990 by Elaine
Steinbeck, Thom Steinbeck, and John Steinbeck IV. Used by permission of Viking Penguin, a division of
Penguin Group (USA) Inc. TURNMIRE, GAIL. "Love Finds the Way" from *Dog Fancy*, October 2004. Used by
permission of Gail Turnmire.

All other stories were previously published in *Angels On Earth* or *Guideposts* magazine or books. Copyright
© by Guideposts, Carmel, NY.

All possible care has been taken to fully acknowledge the ownership and use of the selections in this book.
If any mistakes or omissions have occurred, they will be corrected in subsequent editions, provided notifica-
tion is sent to the publisher.

CONTENTS

My Dog,

My Teacher

At Home Again

Shari Smyth

A chill March wind swept over me as I stood on the deck behind our new house. I stared into the bare woods, longing for a pond, a weather-beaten barn, a field of tall grass, for something familiar—for home. But home was one thousand miles away, in South Salem, New York, where we had raised our four children, where I thought I would live till the end of my days.

Then a serious downturn in my husband's business had forced us to pull up stakes. Whitney and I sold our roomy 1870s colonial and moved to Kingston Springs, Tennessee, a town outside Nashville. Whitney's brother lived nearby, and the cost of living was manageable.

Our new, smaller house sat atop a ridge called Mount Pleasant. With its old-fashioned front porch and dormer windows, I had to admit the place had charm. Whitney insisted the town did too. "Just wait," he said. "Once you settle in, you're going to love it here."

That had happened for him—Mr. Instant Adjustment. He set up his desk and computer in the basement and soon was doing marketing and communications work again. He was glad to give up the hassle of commuting to an office.

It was different for me. I didn't have a job, with its day-to-day routines, to get me grounded. I didn't have anyone to talk to who understood what I was going through. Whitney tried, but he didn't seem to miss South Salem the way I did. He was enchanted with Kingston Springs. "Everyone's so friendly," he marveled. True, but their laid-back attitudes only made me more aware of how uptight I was by comparison. I got tense merely thinking about going into town and facing a bunch of strangers. "God, I just want to go home," I said, sighing. All my prayers seemed to be for the same thing.

I turned from the backyard and looked at our dogs, Roscoe and Chaucer, lolling on the deck. "Wish I could settle in like you guys," I told them.

Whitney stepped outside, taking a break from work. "Why don't you try jogging?" he suggested. "Bring Roscoe with you. You'll get to know the neighborhood." He rubbed my shoulders. "The neighbors too."

Back home I'd had a regular five-mile route. Here I never saw runners on the road, so I had hesitated to start. With one of the dogs for company, though, maybe it wouldn't be so bad.

The next morning, I fastened a collar around Roscoe's thick neck. I barely had time to clip on a leash before he—eighty-five pounds of exuberant Labrador retriever—took off, dragging me down the block. When I went to the grocery store later that day, an older gentleman guffawed and said, "Saw your dog running away with ya." I slipped out quickly with my purchases, resolving not to give folks any more to laugh at.

Spring arrived and I ran alone. I passed people working in their gardens, washing their cars, sitting on their porches chatting with neighbors. Their curious glances made me feel as if my feet were on backward. I ducked my head and kept going. One day I slowed to a walk halfway up Mount Pleasant Road. Near the top of the hill, I noticed a man looking out from his doorway. Taking a chance, I waved. I thought I saw him glare at me and frown. Picking up my pace, I hurried on.

The days grew uncomfortably warm, giving me a convenient excuse to work out to exercise videos indoors. Whitney was worried when he saw me staying in the house. "You're never going to meet anyone this way," he said gently.

I brushed him off. "I'm not used to the heat, that's all," I said, remembering that man's disapproving frown and retreating still deeper into myself and my homesickness.

One evening that summer I got a call from our daughter, Sanna, in Florida. "You know that dog I found last month—Leah?" she asked. (Sanna had inherited my love of animals.) She'd come upon the pup whimpering at the scene of a car accident that killed her owner, who had just adopted her from the pound. When the man's relatives didn't want the dog, Sanna took her in. But Sanna's new job had longer hours. "I won't be able to keep Leah," she said. "I don't know what to do, Mom. None of my friends can take her, and the thought of her going back to the pound—"

"I'll come get her." I could start driving south the next day.

"Mom, thank you!" Sanna exclaimed. "Now I know Leah will have a good home."

All the way to Florida I wondered what had come over me. *We don't have room in the house for three dogs,* I thought. *We can't afford more vet bills. And more to the point: I'm having a hard enough time as it is. What can I do for Leah?* But I'd promised, and I couldn't let my daughter down.

When I met Leah, she was sticking to Sanna's heels, as if that were her rightful place. The half-grown pup was shy and kind of funny looking, with kangaroo ears that seemed the wrong size for her head.

Standing in the driveway before I left, Sanna gave Leah one last hug, then told me, "I think you're going to be good for each other, Mom." I wished I could be so sure.

I climbed in my van for the long drive to Tennessee. Although I'd pulled out the middle seat so Leah would have a place to lie down, she was hiding way in the back, head buried beneath her paws, body shaking as if she were crying. *Maybe the sound of my voice will soothe her.*

"Don't be sad, little girl," I said. "You'll like it where we're going."

Leah didn't look up. "You'll have two big brothers to play with," I continued, "a nice lawn to run around, . . . "

She lay in the same position, tail tucked tight under her. When I ran out of reassurances for her, I kept talking. "I've lost my home too," I said. "Uprooted like you.

"I just want to wake up one day and find myself back where everything's familiar. Where I know the streets, the people, and—" My voice broke. "And they know me." All the emotion I'd bottled up came spilling out.

"I can't go on feeling this miserable," I said, wiping my tears. "Something's got to change. But I don't know what it is."

A wet nose brushed my elbow. I looked down. Leah was between the front seats, peering up at me. Her wistful brown eyes seemed to say, *I know how you feel.*

Leah inched forward, and with a sigh, leaned her head against my leg trustingly. She'd lost one owner tragically, and she was moving to her fourth home in as many months. Yet there she was, willing to try again. Willing to start over.

Is that what I've been missing, Lord? Willingness? I had gone through the motions of making Kingston Springs my home, but deep down I had never wanted it to be. I hadn't given the town—or myself—a chance. I'd clung to the past so stubbornly that, in a way, I'd never really moved to Tennessee.

I rested my hand on Leah's head. "If you're ready to try, I am too," I said. "Maybe together we can make Kingston Springs home."

Whitney fell for her right away. Even Roscoe and Chaucer didn't mind having an excitable puppy in their midst. Leah loved the big guys. But she stuck closest to me—a faithful shadow wherever I went.

Early one evening when summer started giving way to fall, I decided to take Leah running. She kept up with me, and her friendliness seemed to make us both approachable.

"Nice dog," a boy said shyly from the edge of his yard. "Can I pet her?"

"Sure." I waved tentatively at his mother digging in her flower bed.

She waved back and asked, "You doin' all right?"

"I'm getting there," I answered honestly.

"That's what counts," she said, smiling.

I smiled too and resumed my jog, Leah trotting ahead. I came to the top of Mount Pleasant Road, where the frowning man lived. He was out by his mailbox. As my feet pounded the pavement, he lifted his head, squinting. Then I realized how wrong I'd been. He had never glared at me. He was nearly blind. "Hello," I said.

He turned toward me. "You sure must be tired after that long climb."

"If you want to level this road, that's fine by me," I joked.

He laughed. "I'll get right on it."

Leah and I jogged back to our house. I filled her water bowl and brought it out on the deck so we could cool down together. Finishing my stretches, I stood at the railing for a moment and looked out into the woods, the leaves on the trees burnished gold by the fading light.

"Well, little girl, what do you think?" I asked, scratching the top of Leah's head. "It's good to be home, isn't it?"

Her tail thumped.

Joanna's
Remarkable Journey

Anita Wells

My friend Anita Allen and I shared not only the same first name but a love for salukis, those long-legged gazelle hounds, said to be the oldest breed of dog in the world. Several thousand years ago the saluki was the royal dog of ancient Egypt—and indeed Joanna, a fuzzy six-week-old puppy, had regal airs from the first day she arrived in Anita's home in San Antonio, Texas.

Joanna grew into a tall, elegant animal with a handsome red-gold coat and distinctive charcoal markings below her eyes. Anita doted on her. It was as if the dog were a member of her family. That's why I could hardly believe it when Anita told me she had given Joanna away—she didn't even say to whom. The dog was about 250 miles away in Dallas.

Puzzling over this news, I stepped outside my home, where my own salukis bounded up to greet me—I was raising fifteen at the time. As I refilled their water bowls, I recalled the day I first encountered these canine aristocrats. Oh, I had seen them at dog shows, but a saluki at a show is a dispirited animal, droop-eared, tuck-tailed, long, narrow head hung low. Shy with strangers, the saluki sulks in a corner. It was when a breeder invited me to visit the ranch where he raised salukis that I saw them in their natural state: racing to greet him, silky ears streaming, feathery tails aloft like banners. I had been hopelessly, totally, and forever hooked.

I didn't spend too long pondering Anita's news, because soon more pressing worries occupied my mind. I was diagnosed with cancer, and two surgeries failed to halt the fast-spreading disease. Doctors gave me less than a year to live.

I was recovering from surgery when an odd story made the rounds of saluki owners. A woman driving to work on Fredericksburg Road in San Antonio had seen a limping, half-starved dog. She thought it was a saluki—but it couldn't be, we all agreed. No saluki had been reported missing. The woman, though, was sure. A reddish dog, she said, with dark face markings.

Like Joanna, I thought.

But Joanna was in Dallas. Obviously the woman had simply seen some large, slender dog—part Afghan, maybe. Had I been well, I might have tried to find the poor creature. As it was, I could barely walk.

Then why, ill as I was, did I keep hearing over and over, *It's all right.* All right? What was all right? Not my health. Surgery had only eased the pain, not checked the cancer. Then other thoughts: *Trust. Come. Don't be afraid.* Was it— my mind balked at the idea—God? It didn't seem possible. My childhood experiences had convinced me that the people who talked most about God were the ones who cared least about animals. I didn't want to be like that.

In January 1982, in the midst of my health crisis, my friend Anita was diagnosed with a brain tumor. The doctors said it was too late to save her life. Her decline was swift and her death so sudden I could barely take it in.

I was reeling from this tragedy when the saluki grapevine buzzed a second time. The same woman had again caught sight of the injured dog near Fredericksburg Road; once more she insisted it was a saluki. *Joanna!* I thought of Anita's strange announcement, three years earlier, that she had given Joanna away.

What if Anita's thinking had already been confused? Doctors said the tumor had been growing for a long time. Maybe that was why she had given her beloved dog away. Or, more likely, that was the excuse she came up with after the dog accidentally got out.

Friends now argued that this dog could not be Joanna. It would mean a high-strung, shy animal had somehow survived for three years in urban San Antonio. Nevertheless, a dozen of us fanned out across the north side of town. I was able to join the effort, as I was feeling stronger and even driving again. We combed the streets, knocked on doors, posted Joanna's description in shop windows.

Weeks passed with no success. And yet those strange words of reassurance came stronger now than ever: *Trust. Don't be afraid.* Daily, through my own monologue of grief for Anita and fear for myself, the words came: *It's all right.* Slowly I began to believe those words. I would be all right.

Then in April word came that the owner of a beauty

parlor on Fredericksburg Road had seen a dog that fit our description. I phoned my friend Robbie West, who had known Joanna too, and asked her to meet me at the address with a dog cage. The beauty parlor was located in what had once been a private home. Yes, the owner said, the dog he had seen had long legs and a long tail. He didn't see how we could be interested in such a wretched animal, but we were welcome to take it. He had spotted it slinking into the crawlspace beneath the house as he locked up at night.

Why did I sense that this creature was Joanna? *It's all right.* Maybe the dog would be all right too.

Robbie and I walked around the house. The crawlspace was no more than two feet high, with an opening big enough for a large dog to go through. We sat in Robbie's car, watching the house. Dusk came, then dark.

It was Robbie who whispered, "There! Look!" Something slipped into the bushes beside the house. We waited a little longer, then crept from the car, bent down, and shone a flashlight into the crawlspace. Six feet away two glowing eyes shone back. In the circle of light was a dog with a matted red-gold coat. Below the eyes, unmistakable charcoal markings.

"Joanna!" Robbie and I cried.

As we dragged the cage in front of the opening, the dog backed away under the house. *Now what? How do we coax a terrified animal from her hiding place?* For more than an hour we whistled and called her name. "One of us," I said at last, "is going to have to crawl under there."

"You go," Robbie said quickly. "You know salukis."

I knew salukis. I also knew myself. I was claustrophobic, terrified of spiders, and though doctors were dumbfounded at my returning health, still not strong. But Joanna was beneath that house.

We found a long stick and tied a leash to one end, with a loop hanging down to form a lasso. Robbie pulled the cage aside. With the flashlight in one hand and the stick in the other, I flattened myself on my stomach and squirmed through the opening.

Cowering in the farthest corner was Joanna. With my elbows, inch by inch, I dragged myself toward her, fighting panic as the bottom of the house pressed me into the dirt. Cobwebs broke across my face. *Don't think of scorpions. Don't think of tarantulas. Think of a lonely, scared dog.*

Crouched low in the shallow space, Joanna backed away along the wall. "Don't be afraid," I called softly. With each move of mine, Joanna cringed. I hunched forward six inches; she backed away twelve. My body pulsed with pain; my throat was raw with dust. I kept talking. "It's all right. Come, Joanna! Don't be afraid." The frightened animal continued to back away.

"All right, Joanna," I said at last, "what do you want?"

And as clearly as if it were there in front of me, I saw in my mind a pillow—a fluffy, feathery pillow. I pictured its softness. "You'll have that pillow, Joanna," I said. "That's a promise."

I pulled myself forward, and this time Joanna didn't move. Tense, trembling, she watched the loop draw close. Then it was over her head.

Scuttling backward on my elbows, I hauled myself slowly toward the opening, where Robbie waited. Joanna followed the tug of the leash, needing to be drawn but not really struggling. At last I maneuvered the dog into the cage and Robbie slid the door shut.

All the way home I talked to Joanna, who sat in the cage on the seat beside me. "A bath first, Joanna, for both of us. Then the softest pillow you've ever felt."

An hour later, bathed, Joanna and I stood in my bedroom. I had planned to place a pillow at leash-length on the floor, but she was eyeing the one on the bed. She looked at me, then back at the bed, and again at me. I nodded, and up she sprang.

The weary dog was asleep at once, but I lay awake, attached by a strip of leather to an animal who had taken the risk of trust. *We're connected in more ways than you know, Joanna*, I thought. As I had been seeking Joanna, hadn't God been seeking me? Gently, patiently: *Come. Trust. It's all right.* Two of God's creatures slept on pillows that night. Two who were lost no longer.

Belle

Marjorie Holmes

We all knew our dog was doomed. After three long months in the hospital and three operations, she was getting no better. And it was all my fault. Nobody blamed me, yet I felt so guilty.

"If Belle's got to be put to sleep," I insisted that awful morning of our decision, "I'm the one who should give the order."

In vain they tried to spare me. "Mom, no, you don't have to. I will," a son volunteered, before plunging forlornly off to school. My husband said he'd do it from the office. But I was adamant. I should have tied her up before we took off in our boat to pull those water-skiers. I should have watched out for her. After all, I was driving the boat the day we hit her.

The family was finally out of the house. I paced the floor, struggling for composure. *Get it over with. It should be a relief.* We'd been debating this so long . . . I strode to the phone at last. "Doctor Mosseller? We've decided the most merciful thing would be to . . . let Belle go."

"Yes. Okay. I think you're right."

I hung up, drew a deep breath, turned the fire higher under the coffeepot. *Don't cry any more; you've cried enough. She'll be so much better off. Drink your coffee, read the paper. . . .*

but, oh, Belle, forgive me! New and more terrible tears suddenly blurred the page. I sprang up, appalled. I felt like an executioner, as if I had just ordered that one of my own children be put to death—or at least a whole era in the life of our family. Even as I raced back to the phone, I was crying out loud, "No, no! What have I done?"

This time the circuits were busy. I dialed again and again. Finally the doctor's aide was saying, "I'll see if I can catch him . . ." Then the doctor himself was on the line.

"Stop, wait, don't do it!" I gasped.

In the silence that followed, my heart almost stopped. "You caught me just in time," he said. "Are you sure?"

"Yes. No! . . . Yes, it's got to be done, but wait till tonight, please. At least we can come down and tell her goodbye."

A bit sheepishly I called my husband then—and he agreed. "But let's not say anything more to the kids," he said. "They've accepted it; no use putting them through it all again."

As we drove the forty miles to the small Virginia town where we had our summer cabin, we reminisced about Belle.

This fat, polka-dotted Dalmatian had been an oddball from puppyhood. Her eyes didn't match—by day, one was blue, one brown, and after dark they lit up like stoplights, red and green. She barked; she shed; she luxuriated on forbidden sofas, raided trash cans, and ate everything that didn't eat her first.

And how she loved to swim. She was always first in the car when we headed for the lake, and the first one out, streaking for the water like a jubilant child. The skiers learned to swoop around her eagerly chugging head.

Then we got a new boat—a new secondhand boat, rather—but bigger and more powerful than our last. The teenagers wanted to try it out that evening. I said I'd drive. I had a strange feeling I really ought to tie Belle up. But, sensing excitement, she was already dashing past us. We heard the usual big splash as she dived in.

I forgot all about her. It was enough just to concentrate on the controls, to watch and listen for the signals from my husband and the tensely waiting skiers.

"Hit it!" The traditional call from skiers ready to take off.

I pulled back the lever, we shot through the water. . . . then that body-shattering jolt. That awful thud. Those wild, agonized yelps.

The details of that dreadful night came back to me so clearly. Our frantic calls to vets until we reached one who would see her if we'd bring her in. But we'd have to detour, we were told—there was a parade. Then there was the dash through the countryside—a daughter driving while the rest of us cradled and tried to comfort the blanket-wrapped bundle in the back of the station wagon. Despite the long, bumpy detour, we ran into the parade. Our daughter jumped out, dripping wet, and begged a policeman to let us through. He shook his head and turned his back. We traveled more desperate miles, only to encounter more parade.

The car stopped. "Here, Daddy, you drive." Again Melanie leaped from the car and, extending both arms, simply stopped the parade until we could pass.

Doctor Mosseller couldn't give us much hope. "I'll try to

make her comfortable. If she makes it till morning we may be able to operate, but even then . . ."

Belle made it all through the summer, while that brilliant young vet put her mangled body back together. But one leg refused to heal. More operations loomed—a bone graft, perhaps, but even that would be arduous and doubtful. Amputation would probably be best. We winced at the prospect. Poor Belle—could she stand it? Could we? . . .

Then we were at the vet's office. We could hear Belle barking clear down the corridor, as if she sensed our presence. They wheeled her out on a little cart—and her tail was wagging! Wildly, eagerly, despite the cast and bandages, she greeted us, quivering, contorting in an ecstatic frenzy. People have words to express their love; dogs can only strain and wag and frantically lick your hands.

We knew we couldn't put her away. And the doctor read the message in the tears that ran down our faces. "Look, if you're willing to nurse her, why not take her home until you're sure?"

Rejoicing, we lifted her into the car.

The youngsters couldn't believe it—the dead restored. They were beside themselves. They helped with the nursing, and the spoiling. For she was queen of the family now, reigning from the once-forbidden sofa—this former, often scolded renegade. But we knew we had only postponed the inevitable, and it haunted us. Especially the weekend we took her to the lake, and she lay whimpering, gazing toward the water.

It was at that point I remembered the words in the Bible,

"Where two or three are gathered together . . ." (Matthew 18:20). Why not try prayer? My column "Love and Laughter" was appearing in the *Washington Star*. I would ask not only our church and our friends but my readers also to gather in a common spiritual purpose. And so I told the story of Belle, concluding: "The verdict is this. In another month, if the hip has not healed—amputation, or the end. There are no accounts in Scripture of the healing of animals. But I believe the Good Shepherd would have healed a pet had he been asked."

The newspaper was scarcely on the street when the telephone began to ring. Prayer circles. Animal shelters. Individuals. Then came the avalanche of mail. "The Lord is concerned about everything that is dear to us," one letter said. "He knows every sparrow that falls," another wrote. People shared their experiences, funny and sad. They advised, told of successful amputations. Above all, they told us they were praying.

As for Belle, had she any idea of the flood of love she had released? We can never know. We know only that as she stretched and scrambled around, she became less awkward with the cast, then surprisingly nimble. Two weeks later, when we went back to the doctor, he was amazed. "There's still a lot of damage. The pin has shifted. . . . but the tissue is growing!" By the third week he was able to lessen the bindings; by the fourth, to remove the cast altogether.

"It's remarkable," he said. "She'll have some arthritis, but she'll be swimming again next summer. This dog is well!"

Belle lived three more years—still battle-scarred, a little gimpy. And as she would stand, her hips in perfect alignment, I remembered what one reader urged. "Never offer God a picture of injury. Visualize perfection."

And with the living proof of that philosophy before me, I sometimes thought that maybe if we all visualized perfection and kept the image vivid, our lives and the whole world would be more perfect. And if all of us would pray for each other with the selfless warmth and enthusiasm with which people prayed for Belle, miracles could occur every day.

The Existence
of Dog

Elena Sigman

My year-old son, Isaiah, can sense an approaching dog. If the dog is a block away or across the street, Isaiah's little back jolts upright, his arms extend and flap, and he tries to propel himself into the air, a dog-copter. His breath comes out in rapid sighs, *eh-eh-eh*. I push the stroller faster, fearful that the dog's master, oblivious to this drama, will steer his four-legged mate in another direction, and my son's heart will break. But no, we catch up with the dog, Isaiah leaps up, straining against the stroller's strap: "Ahhhhyyyiii!"

This instinctive attraction to dogs is the first significant way in which my child is different from me. There are many other things we do not share that might seem more important, including gender. But this strikes me as a very big difference: Isaiah loves dogs. He always has, and his love for them just keeps growing stronger.

I have never liked dogs. It's not just that I don't have a dog myself; until a year ago, I ignored them out of existence. They didn't live in the same three dimensions that I inhabited. They occupied their own dog world, a planet of poops, pooper-scoopers, and pooper-leavers; a planet of bark-ing and biting, endless noises and secretions.

Now, suddenly, I have a child who is a dog lover, dog watcher, dog stopper, dog dogger. Dog is on Isaiah's mind even when a dog is not in sight. He is ready, prepared at all times for an encounter. He loves to get in the stroller, tolerates the belting in and sweatering up and whatever else must be gotten through in order to go outside. He longs to greet the world, knowing that the world is filled with dogs. He goes out, arms flung open and willing.

At first, I was skeptical. The passion that provoked Isaiah to crow with delight at the approach of a shaggy canine was completely foreign to me. But now, I am won over. I have wit-nessed the dog's heart-stopping hello, the wet nose, the long tongue meeting Isaiah's for a quick kiss. I have smelled the var-ious fur smells of wet, dry, oily, and hot dogs; seen a paw lifted in greeting, a tail draped provocatively across the bar of Isaiah's stroller like a cabaret singer's boa resting on a man's shoulder.

I have discovered the thrill of anticipating a dog, the excitement in the mere idea of a dog. Down any block, around any corner, exists the prospect of comfort, love, welcome, wet eyes, velvet muzzles, deep, deep fur to lose your fingers in; the possibility of nose pulls, yowps, tongue rolls, fists of fur, ear flicks, paw dances, a brush with ecstasy. Perhaps, for the dog, it's all about salt; for Isaiah, it's all about love. Love for some-thing animated, roughly his own height, that runs to him as he runs to it. It? No, not an it. Not a he or a she either. A supreme being.

The power of Isaiah's joy is so strong that I am converted. I believe in dog, and in this heightened, devotional consciousness, I too seek out dogs wherever I go. I am not so much a human being, woman, or mother as a dog finder. The extra three feet of height that I have over Isaiah is an adaptive trait that has evolved so I can spot dogs from farther away.

I know things now that I never knew I could know: I know that basset hounds have the long ears that drop like tablecloths to the ground. I know who's a mutt and who's not. I know that in a cocker-poodle mix, the brains come from the poodle side of the family.

Day by day, we log more encounters of the doggie kind: We pass a couple sitting on a bench, a dog sitting on his haunches between them. Isaiah's dog-alert goes off, the arms whirring up and down, the siren of delight, and the woman in this couple falls in love with my son.

"Here, want to feed Coco?" she asks. She gives Isaiah a dog biscuit. He holds it out to the dog, who licks it up. He laughs as the dog keeps licking, licking his empty hand and his wrist all the way to the elbow and beyond. Isaiah shrieks with pleasure and holds his hand out like a prize. Even after the couple leaves and the dog's tail wags away, he holds his dog-licked arm up like a trophy.

Why didn't I like dogs for so many years? Fear. And why, for so many years, didn't I want to have a baby? Fear. When I was a child, growing up in Los Angeles, a huge red dog lived behind my house. On my side of a very short chainlink fence grew some agapanthus and jade plants; on the other side was a fierce, salivating, jaw-snapping attack machine. I feared being eaten by that dog.

As an adult, I outgrew my fear of being eaten by a dog, but not the fear of being consumed. People with dogs, and babies, love them beyond measure. They are consumed with love. I never believed that I could survive such inordinate passion.

When I was a child, I never asked to have a dog. I thought that dogs were dirty, noisy, mean. I also believed that there was not enough time, energy, or space (love) in our house for children and a dog. What no one told me, until my husband mentioned it, is that love breeds more love. Love of a dog just makes room for more love. My husband can, it now appears, love me and our baby. More marvelous: I too love them both.

There is, of course, a developmental explanation for the phenomenon of dog love in both Isaiah's life and mine. The rationalist will point to Isaiah's growing capacity to retrieve memories over the course of his first year of life. Isaiah is not simply experiencing dog for the first time, over and over, but linking memories and fitting them into the concept of dog. Thanks to object permanence, Isaiah has, from six months, known that dogs do not cease to exist when he cannot see them.

I too have entered a new developmental phase, in which the ability to love a dog is connected to the experience of generativity that pulled me into parenthood. Yet science cannot explain everything. I managed to avoid my biological destiny for two decades, and might have avoided it permanently.

Instead, I have taken a leap of faith. I am listening to the part of me that says: *Let's try it, let's see what happens.* I feared I would not be even remotely decent as a mother. Now I am doing the thing I cannot do perfectly and loving myself a bit, loving Isaiah all the more. Why is it that I didn't see dogs before? I think I didn't know, didn't want to know, that I am like a dog, out in the world looking for scraps of food, warmth, and love, maybe some shade on a hot day.

Now I live in dogs' world; and I can sense that there is a dog out there now, already smiling, a bit of drool coming off his long tongue, waiting for me to notice and smile back.

Travels with Charley

John Steinbeck

I must confess to a laxness in the matter of national parks. I haven't visited many of them. Perhaps this is because they enclose the unique, the spectacular, the astounding—the greatest waterfall, the deepest canyon, the highest cliff, the most stupendous works of man or nature. And I would rather see a good Brady photograph than Mount Rushmore. For it is my opinion that we enclose and celebrate the freaks of our nation and of our civilization. Yellowstone National Park is no more representative of America than is Disneyland.

This being my natural attitude, I don't know what made me turn sharply south and cross a state line to take a look at Yellowstone. Perhaps it was a fear of my neighbors. I could hear them say, "You mean you were that near to Yellowstone and didn't go? You must be crazy." Again it might have been the American tendency in travel. One goes not so much to see, but to tell afterward. Whatever my purpose in going to Yellowstone, I'm glad I went, because I discovered something about Charley that I might never have known.

A pleasant-looking national-park man checked me in

and then he said, "How about that dog? They aren't permitted in except on leash."

"Why?" I asked.

"Because of the bears."

"Sir," I said, "this is an unique dog. He does not live by tooth or fang. He respects the right of cats to be cats although he doesn't admire them. He turns his steps rather than disturb an earnest caterpillar. His greatest fear is that someone will point out a rabbit and suggest that he chase it. This is a dog of peace and tranquility. I suggest that the greatest danger to your bears will be pique at being ignored by Charley."

The young man laughed. "I wasn't so much worried about the bears," he said. "But our bears have developed an intolerance for dogs. One of them might demonstrate his prejudice with a clip on the chin, and then—no dog."

"I'll lock him in the back, sir. I promise you Charley will cause no ripple in the bear world, and as an old bear-looker, neither will I."

"I just have to warn you," he said. "I have no doubt your dog has the best of intentions. On the other hand, our bears have the worst. Don't leave food about. Not only do they steal, but they are critical of anyone who tries to reform them. In a word, don't believe their sweet faces or you might get clobbered. And don't let the dog wander. Bears don't argue."

We went on our way into the wonderland of nature gone nuts, and you will have to believe what happened. The only way I can prove it would be to get a bear.

Less than a mile from the entrance, I saw a bear beside

the road; and it ambled out as though to flag me down. Instantly a change came over Charley. He shrieked with rage. His lips flared, showing wicked teeth that have some trouble with a dog biscuit. He screeched insults at the bear, which hearing, the bear reared up and seemed to me to overtop *Rocinante*, [my camper-truck]. Frantically I rolled the windows shut and, swinging quickly to the left, grazed the animal, then scuttled on while Charley raved and ranted beside me, describing in detail what he would do to that bear if he could get at him. I was never so astonished in my life. To the best of my knowledge Charley had never seen a bear, and in his whole history had showed great tolerance for every living thing. Besides all this, Charley is a coward, so deep-seated a coward that he has developed a technique for concealing it. And yet he showed every evidence of wanting to get out and murder a bear that outweighed him a thousand to one. I don't understand it.

A little farther along two bears showed up, and the effect was doubled. Charley became a maniac. He leaped all over me, he cursed and growled, snarled and screamed. I didn't know he had the ability to snarl. Where did he learn it? Bears were in good supply, and the road became a nightmare. For the first time in his life Charley resisted reason, even resisted a cuff on the ear. He became a primitive killer lusting for the blood of his enemy, and up to this moment he had had no enemies. In a bearless stretch, I opened the cab, took Charley by the collar, and locked him in the house. But that did no good. When we passed other bears, he leaped on the table and scratched at the windows trying to get out at them. I could hear canned goods crashing as he struggled in his mania. Bears simply brought out the Hyde in my Jekyll-headed dog. What could have caused it? I know him well. Once in a while he tries a bluff, but it is a palpable lie. I swear that this was no lie. I am certain that if he were released he would have charged every bear we passed and found victory or death.

It was too nerve-wracking, a shocking spectacle, like seeing an old, calm friend go insane. No amount of natural wonders, of rigid cliffs and belching waters, of smoking springs could even engage my attention while that pandemonium went on. After about the fifth encounter, I gave up, turned *Rocinante* about, and retraced my way. If I had stopped for the night and bears had gathered to my cooking, I dare not think what would have happened.

At the gate the park guard checked me out. "You didn't stay long. Where's the dog?"

"Locked up back there. And I owe you an apology. That dog has the heart and soul of a bear-killer and I didn't know it. Heretofore he has been a little tender-hearted toward an underdone steak."

"Yeah!" he said. "That happens sometimes. That's why I warned you. A bear dog would know his chances, but I've seen a Pomeranian go up like a puff of smoke. You know, a well-favored bear can bat a dog like a tennis ball."

I moved fast, back the way I had come, and I was reluctant to camp for fear that there might be some unofficial non-government bears about. That night I spent in a pretty auto court near Livingston. I had my dinner in a restaurant, and when I had settled in with a drink and a comfortable chair and my bathed bare feet on a carpet with red roses, I inspected Charley. He was dazed. His eyes held a faraway look and he was totally exhausted, emotionally no doubt. He couldn't eat his dinner, he refused the evening walk, and once we were in, he collapsed on the floor and went to sleep. In the night I heard him whining and yapping; and when I turned on the light, his feet were making running gestures and his body jerked and his eyes were wide open, but it was only a night bear. I awakened him and gave him some water. This time he went to sleep and didn't stir all night. In the morning he was still tired. I wonder why we think that the thoughts and emotions of animals are simple.

Growing Pains

Shari Smyth

I look at Roscoe sleeping sweetly in his crate, his paws twitching as he dreams. I wonder what a seven-week-old Labrador retriever pup dreams about. I envy him that his morning has been so peaceful while mine is shaping up as a minor nightmare. As it usually does these days, the trouble began with my thirteen-year-old son, Jonathan.

It started when I caught him dropping globs of hair gel on my antique mahogany table while using the mirror above it.

"If I've told you once, I've told you a thousand times . . ." I exploded. Once again we were bickering—me nagging and controlling, my son resentful and defiant. Hearing the whine of the school bus outside, I rudely pushed him out the door. I noticed Jonathan's thin shoulders sagging a little as he ran. *Good*, I thought, *maybe I've gotten through to him this time.*

Then later this morning came *another* call from the dean of students at my son's junior high school.

"Mrs. Smyth," he began hesitantly, "I know you've probably come to dread these reports as much as I do, but we've had another incident here you must be told about."

What now? I wondered helplessly. My mind raced over

the catalog of recent transgressions Jonathan had committed. He hadn't always been like this.

"In science class this morning," the dean said, clearing his throat, "Jonathan was carrying on and sprayed another boy's shirt with iodine. He must stay for detention; and, of course, that shirt will have to be paid for."

My face burned with embarrassment and rage as I hung up the phone. The money Jonathan had been saving for new hockey gear would now go for the boy's shirt. That much I knew. But I was at a loss to understand what was happening to Jonathan, or what to do about it. Jonathan's adolescence had hit us like a tidal surge. When I wasn't quarreling with Jonathan, I was worrying about him, resenting this newfound obnoxiousness.

I try to shake off the mornings traumas and turn my attention back to the slumbering Roscoe. He has a public appearance to make. Roscoe is a Guiding Eyes puppy, and I have agreed to raise him until he's ready for formal guide-dog training. I was warned by his breeders that he was the dominant pup of his litter and will be a real handful once he begins to assert himself. So far he has been a dream.

An hour later I am seated on a folding chair in front of an elementary school gymnasium filled with giggling, squirming children. They crane their heads for a peek at the sleek puppy on my lap. Roscoe's dark eyes casually scan his little fans. I glance at the grown-up guide dog sitting tall beside her blind owner next to me. "That is what you will be like when you grow up," I whisper into Roscoe's soft puppy-ear. He steals a kiss and wags his tail.

We begin the program with Kathy from Guiding Eyes explaining my role as a puppy raiser. She tells the children that I will steer my dog from puppyhood through adolescence. I am to love and discipline him; teach him manners and basic commands; and, when he is older, take him to public places such as restaurants and office buildings.

While Kathy talks, Roscoe chews his teething ring placidly. The children laugh at him because he has suddenly fallen asleep and is snoring loudly. Roscoe awakes with a start, bewildered, and cocks an ear.

I look out at their fresh-scrubbed faces. They seem so eager and cooperative, like Jonathan before he turned thirteen. There he is in my mind again. Jonathan. I am always brooding about what he used to be like or what I wish he would be like now. It's not so much what he does, but the belligerence he does it with. Yes, sometimes he is the same sweet kid I've always known. Usually he is. But other times he is moody, defiant. I hate the person I am becoming. I always seem to be carrying a grudge against my son, like today. I am anxious for him to come home from school so we can have it out about that boy's shirt.

Roscoe shifts in my lap and I snap back to the program. Audrey, the blind lady, is demonstrating how her dog, Eva, makes it possible for her to live a virtually normal life. The children are hushed with amazement. "Forward!" Audrey commands. Eva confidently leads her through a maze of chairs and around a grand piano. "Good girl!" There is a burst of applause. Roscoe sits up groggily and wags his tail. He believes the clapping is for him.

"No, Roscoe," I say softly. "Someday people will applaud you, but we have a long road ahead of us."

On the way home Roscoe whimpers in his crate. He is demanding to sit on my lap while I drive. This is not the Roscoe who came from the breeder a few days ago.

"No," I say firmly, keeping my eyes on the street.

The whimpering quickly escalates to a high-pitched yowl. I slap the top of the crate with a loud whop. This behavior must be discouraged. Roscoe stops—temporarily. We battle all the way home, and I begin to understand the breeder's warning. Roscoe is a strong-willed pup!

After lunch I can't find Roscoe. I call his name and whistle. Suddenly I hear a terrible racket in the next room and race toward it. Roscoe has cornered Sheba, our cat, who deftly springs to a table. "Roscoe, no!" I yell, joining the chase. Ignoring my command, Roscoe bounds after her, bouncing up and down from the floor. *Crash.* My beautiful African violets in their prized, hand-painted vase splatter in a broken mess. Roscoe, the unrepentant, dives gleefully through the dirt, smearing it into the rug. I am appalled by his behavior. "Bad dog!" I shout.

His eyes gleam up at me triumphantly, challenging me. I think back to what the puppy manual advises about dominance. Be firm, it says, be patient. And always follow punishment with praise. Roscoe complies with my order to sit. Then I praise him to the skies. He is his old puppy self again.

I scoop him up and return him to his crate. Immediately he begins to whine; soon it is a full-blown tantrum. I need some peace, so I head off to the library. I won't be gone long. I want to be back when Jonathan gets home. I haven't forgotten what happened in science class.

When I return I hear Roscoe still carrying on upstairs. My temper is about to explode. It blows sky-high when I reach the crate. Roscoe has completely torn apart his little domain. I yank him out of the crate, put him down on the floor and yell something I don't mean: "You will never, ever make it as a guide dog! I don't want you anymore!"

This time Roscoe hangs his head in shame. His ears draw back and his tail droops. He is truly sorry. But I am still angry with his willfulness. He must learn to control himself. "You can't keep testing me like this," I complain. As I stomp away, Roscoe follows meekly at my heels. He won't let me out of his sight. It strikes me that the little puppy needs me more now than ever. He seems to understand this somehow.

Suddenly a phrase from another manual comes to mind, the "manual" of love:

"Love never gives up."

It is from 1 Corinthians 13, and it is just another way of saying that love always gives second chances. How many have I had from God? Too many to count!

"Love does not keep a record of wrongs." Another line from 1 Corinthians. I stop and look out the window. In the distance I see the school bus making its way up the street. I've been wrangling with Roscoe all day long, but deep in my heart I have also been wrangling with Jonathan, fighting the resentment that was left hanging in the air after our argument this morning, resentment I have not let go of. I have been keeping a record, a bitter record, of all of my son's wrongs.

Jonathan, I think, is trying to find his feet in life. It is a process we all go through, and it is not always pleasant. Strangely, in his search for independence, Jonathan needs me more than ever. He needs me to be firm yet patient, to help him find his way through a terribly difficult period. It is a learning process for us both, but he will never again be the little boy he was. He is growing up, and, more than ever, my love must give second chances.

I feel Roscoe leaning comfortably against my ankle. I look down and give him a rub on his head. "I'm sorry," I say. Something in his eyes reveals that he understands me, and he will try to do better.

A few minutes later the front door opens and closes. Jonathan stands in the doorway to the kitchen, tossing his gel-styled hair defiantly. He is braced for a lecture loaded with wrongs from his recent past. I surprise him, and myself. "Why did you do it?" I ask simply.

He studies me silently, then sits down at the table and stares out the window. I strain to hear his answer.

"I don't know," he says. "I just wasn't thinking."

It is an honest answer, not an excuse. He shifts uncomfortably and volunteers that the right thing to do is pay for the shirt with his own money and write an apology.

Before he leaves I feel compelled to say something good about him. When I think about it, it is not hard. There are many, many good things about Jonathan. "Your dad and I appreciate how considerate you are about letting us know where you're going and when you're coming home."

Jonathan looks away in embarrassment and gets up to go to his room and study. As he leaves, I am full of love and pride for my son.

It is nighttime. Roscoe is asleep again, snoring in his little crate. Jonathan comes into the kitchen. He piddles around, then looks at me steadily. "Mom," he says, "I really am sorry."

"Me too," I gulp.

Quickly, before I can hug him, he's off to bed.

Dear Lord, I pray, *thank you for showing me how to wipe the slate clean.*

The Lady
Wore Black

Thomas Peevey

Y ou'd better come home at once," my wife said anxiously from the other end of the phone. "Lady collapsed while eating her supper and can't get up."

"I'll leave right away," I told her. After a quick explanation to my boss, I was leaving for home. Lady had been ailing for several months now, and it was very important that I be there when her time came.

It's funny how memories flood back. On my drive home, I remembered the first time I saw Lady. I had gotten her seventeen years earlier, shortly after my arrival from England. I was working on a small thoroughbred-horse farm near Lexington, Kentucky, and I mentioned to a coworker that I wanted a dog. Carlos smiled and said he knew of a dog for me. A friend of his was leaving for Florida and couldn't take his dog with him.

I met Lady that evening. A dog with a smooth, shiny black coat, pointed ears and muzzle, and a long tail, she weighed about thirty pounds. What was she? I never knew. Maybe a cross between a corgi and a Labrador? A friend thought she might have a bit of schipperke. Lady was never a dog that liked a lot of patting, but she was very knowing. I'm convinced that she sensed my loneliness and took it upon herself to be my protector and companion from day one.

The next morning, Lady followed me down to the barns from my trailer on top of the hill. She'd lie in the corner of each stall as I cleaned them out. She loved to play tug of war with the rope shanks as I went out into the fields to bring the horses in for their feed.

Lady's gaiety and love of life made her a good friend. She would have "puppy fits," running around the fields in big circles, chasing birds, barking and making me laugh. I'll never forget the time when she was playing with two puppies that strayed onto the farm. She ran from them, zigzagging and barking, then looked over her shoulder and did a sudden U-turn between the puppies. In their effort to follow they ran into each other. Lady, tongue hanging out, lay down as if to say, "You guys have a lot to learn!"

Lady loved to swim. On hot days she'd find her way to the farm pond where she'd wallow like a hippo, tongue hanging out, as if to say, "Man, this feels good!" Then she would take off and swim in big circles. When she was finished, she would climb out and shake and roll in the grass.

She was a crafty rascal too. The owner of the farm had some bantam chickens that ran free and would lay their eggs on the tops of the haystacks in the barns, some twenty feet up. Lady found a way to the top, climbed from bale to bale, and brought the eggs down gently in her mouth, one at a time. She would carry an egg out to the blacktop road and drop it, breaking it so she could eat the contents.

Late that year, I was having a farewell dinner for a friend who was returning to Ireland. It was late December. The stars glittered against the black sky and it was bitterly cold. My feet crunched on the frost on the wooden deck. I had fired up the charcoal grill that stood on a waist-high stand outside my trailer, and Lady watched me intently as I placed four pork chops over the white-hot coals. I waited a few minutes, then turned the chops.

My toes were freezing, so I popped back into the trailer to warm my feet. Lady preferred being out in the cold and stayed behind. A few minutes later, I came back to check on the chops. To my dismay, I found only three chops. Lady was lying next to the grill, contentedly licking her lips. I couldn't be cross—I was too impressed by her incredible dexterity, balance, and tenacity. She had retrieved that chop from a white-hot grill that was higher than she was tall. There wasn't even anything that she could have stood on.

When Lady was about six years old, I got a second dog, a Jack Russell terrier I called Betsy. Betsy and Lady became great friends. Betsy was typical of a Jack Russell, tenacious and joyful. Their personalities complemented each other well.

Soon after, I got a good job on one of the major thoroughbred farms in Kentucky. Life on the new farm was good too. I spent much time driving around the farm in my truck. When the dogs rode in the cab, Lady would sit in the passenger seat while Betsy lay on the seat back, across my shoulders. However, they much preferred riding in the back where they could bark at passing trucks. Lady particularly liked to bite at the trees as we passed. One day, as I drove around the farm, they both jumped out of the moving truck to chase a skunk in the field. Lady, being wiser, avoided being sprayed, but Betsy got doused.

Then disaster struck. Like many farm workers, I lived in a house on the farm. One morning, as I was leaving for work, I let the dogs out the front door as I always did. Betsy must have seen a squirrel or something, because instead of getting in the truck as she always did, she darted across the road and was struck by a farm truck. The driver, one of my best grooms, got out and picked Betsy up. He was visibly distraught as he carried her over to me.

Betsy was still alive, but she was in a bad way, bleeding from the mouth and breathing very heavily. I ushered Lady back into my house. Then the groom and I left to take Betsy to the veterinarian. Unfortunately, Betsy died. I left her at the vet's office, not knowing quite what to do with the body.

When I got back to the farm, I decided that I would go for a long walk to grieve. I took Lady with me. As she got in the cab of the truck, she looked through the back window and then turned to me as if to say, "Where's Betsy?" I hadn't experienced much grief at that time in my life, and I don't think I was aware of Lady's concern.

I drove to Masterson Station Park, a historic plantation outside of Lexington that has been preserved as open fields.

Lady loved going there. She usually ran around barking and chasing birds. This time she stayed close to me, leading me to the back of the park. We walked for miles. I had my head down and was feeling sad when I heard a voice ask, "What's the matter?"

I looked up and saw a well-dressed elderly man in a tweed coat, tie, and cap. He had a trimmed gray beard and a kind face. He reminded me of an old friend back home in Newmarket, England.

Lady sat next to me as I told the man about Betsy. He came over and gave me a gentle hug and said that Betsy wouldn't want me to be sad. I knew he was right. As he walked away, I wondered if God sent him to help me deal with the grief. My family was far away in England and farm life was quite lonely. I wondered if Lady had led me to this spot to meet this elderly gentleman who looked so much like home. After all, what was a man like that doing so far out away from the road?

Lady normally followed me into the house after work. For several weeks after Betsy died, she would stay on the porch as if waiting for Betsy. She eventually gave up, but I'm sure she was always perplexed about Betsy suddenly going missing.

I wanted to get another dog for Lady, and a few months later I got a beagle named Millie. Lady and Millie became great friends. Millie was full of mischief. Raising her, and keeping her out of trouble, eased Lady's grief as well as mine.

Shortly after getting Millie, I lost my job. I was allowed to continue living in my house for two months after being terminated. In that time, I spent quite a bit of time off the farm looking for a new job. I would leave Lady and Millie with Thirza, one of my recently hired grooms. Thirza loved my dogs and took great care of them. She took them to lunch every day and bought them a burger to share. Lady would follow Thirza from stall to stall, as she had with me. At three o'clock each day, she would say goodbye to Thirza and walk up to my house to sit on the porch and wait for me. It was as if she were saying, "You are very nice, but I want to be with my dad."

When Lady was thirteen, I bought my own home and began working at a feed research facility. The dogs continued to go to work with me, and my new boss, Karen, became quite fond of them as well. While I was working there, Lady became very ill. She was weak and wouldn't eat. It took several visits to the vet to diagnose hemolytic anemia, a deadly autoimmune disease in which the body attacks its own red blood cells. It is almost always fatal. When Lady was diagnosed, her red cell count was nine. A count of eight is seen only in a dead dog.

She spent five terrible days and nights in intensive care, but I wasn't ready to say goodbye to my old friend. She barely clung to life, but with transfusions, steroids, and round-the-clock supportive care, her red cell count slowly climbed. I was constantly on the phone to my family in England, giving them updates. Karen inquired daily about her condition as well.

When I was finally able to take Lady home, I asked the receptionist about the bill, telling her I couldn't pay that day. The receptionist smiled and told me that a friend of Lady's had come in to inquire about her and paid one hundred dollars toward the bill, but wouldn't give a name. I later learned the mystery lady was Karen. My father and younger brother, knowing how much I loved Lady, paid the rest. I felt that they were as happy as I that she recovered.

Lady was getting to be an old dog. A year later she had a second bout of hemolytic anemia. At about that time, I met up with Thirza again, and we started going out. Lady seemed to approve of the match. It was almost as if she were trying to find a replacement for herself. "Dad," she seemed to say, "we both know that I'm not going to be here much longer. You need someone to follow you around when I'm gone."

When I asked Thirza to marry me and she accepted, Lady seemed overjoyed. She followed up more closely than usual, as if to share in the joy of the moment. Almost blind and deaf, she looked at me through clouded eyes as if to say, "About time, too! Now you've found someone to love you as much as I do, and I'll be able to go in peace."

All these scenes came crowding back into my memory as I hurried home to be with Lady. On my arrival, I found my wife lying on the floor next to Lady, comforting her. Lady hardly recognized me. I sat next to her on the floor and gently stroked her. She was nearly eighteen years old, and we all knew it was her time.

I rang our vet, knowing he was unable to come to his clinic due to a recent surgery. He sent his partner, Dr. Coutts, and she was wonderful. She met us in the clinic parking lot, and we stood there in the dark, under the stars, while she encouraged me to talk about Lady. That brought mostly laughter, but also tears. It was time.

We entered the clinic, and I gently laid Lady on the table. I was holding her and my wife was holding me as Dr. Coutts inserted the needle. Lady was still, and we were quiet. After a moment, she slipped away.

Dr. Coutts asked if we would like her to dispose of the body. Remembering Lady's reaction to Betsy's disappearance, I said no. I wanted to take her home so our other pets could say goodbye. Dr. Coutts gave us a cardboard casket and helped us place Lady in it.

When we got home, I put the casket in the back room and opened the lid. Millie came first. She minutely sniffed Lady from head to foot. She gave a sigh, went to her basket, and was quiet for the rest of the night. Merry, our tortoiseshell cat, did the same. Then our buff-colored cat, Charlie, gently got into the casket and lay with Lady for some time.

The next day, I buried Lady along with her bowl, her collar, and her leash. The animals seemed content, and we all had closure. Lady had been such a good friend to us. She had helped me to learn about love, loyalty, and just plain having fun.

My Angel

Plays Fetch

"You're a Good
Dog, Tyler"

Diane Quinlan

O kay, Tyler, we're ready for you," the nurse said, smiling at the large golden retriever sitting beside me. She held the conference room door open and beckoned to Tyler. He glanced at me and then led us confidently through the door.

It was an important moment for us. Administrators at the Children's Hospital of Philadelphia were considering the use of dogs as pet therapists, to visit and cheer up sick patients. The animals are specially trained and certified, along with their owners. Studies have shown they can promote the healing and well-being of people in nursing homes, hospitals and rehabilitation centers.

When I was a teenager I once spent six lonely weeks in the hospital for spinal surgery. Visits from family and friends were limited, and no pets were allowed. I remember how good it felt to be back home, where my dog could curl up on my bed beside me. Running my hands through his fur or letting him lick my fingers, I was distracted from my pain. As an adult I became a nurse, and for the past several years I've worked at the Children's Hospital of Philadelphia (or CHOP, as we call it). I had become convinced that a pet-therapy program could comfort the kids in our care.

For months, several other nurses and I pleaded with the hospital administrators. Finally we were told, "Bring the dog in and give us a demonstration."

Before we left our house that day, I gave Tyler a big hug. "It's up to you, boy," I said.

From the beginning there was something exceptional about Tyler. An eighty-five-pound golden retriever, he had a way with people. Gentle and easygoing, he didn't even chew things when he was a puppy. "He's too good to be true," my husband, Jim, had said. That's why, when we registered him with the American Kennel Club, we called him Good As Gold. At home, though, he was always Tyler.

I had big plans for him. He was such a handsome dog, I was certain he would do well in shows. He went to shows with me and placed fourth in his breed at the Westminster Kennel Club Dog Show at Madison Square Garden. Yet something was missing. Good show dogs thrive in the limelight. Not Tyler. One Saturday morning, ready to leave for a show, I called him. For once, he didn't come running. I found him upstairs, snuggled in bed with Jim, looking happier than he ever had in the ring. *You're no show dog, Tyler,* I thought.

But what was he? Attentive and biddable, he did well in obedience school. Wasn't there some way he could use those skills?

When I read a newspaper article about a pet-therapy program, I knew it was the perfect thing. Tyler had always been attuned to my emotions. When I came home from work frustrated with our inability to save a sick child, he would rest his head in my lap until my grief lifted. I could see him doing the same for the kids.

First he had to be tested by a Therapy Dogs International evaluator. He passed with flying colors. All that remained was for me to convince the hospital staff. As we entered the conference room, we faced twelve skeptical doctors in their crisp white coats. Within ten minutes half of them were down on the floor petting Tyler. A few weeks later the pet-therapy program was approved, and Tyler started his new job.

He was a natural. Usually we spent our time in the intensive care unit, where I worked. Some people found it upsetting to see children suffering from trauma or cancer. But Tyler didn't mind if a child was bald, bandaged, or hooked up to a ventilator.

He seemed to sense when a child was afraid of dogs, and he kept his distance, wagging his tail, as if to say, "It's okay. I understand. I like you anyway." If a child held out a hand, Tyler was only too happy to be petted. One little girl who was recovering from surgery reached out to him and started to cry. "She misses her own dog," her mother said. The nurses laid a blanket on the floor and put the child on it so Tyler could lie down next to her. She fell asleep with her fingers curled in Tyler's fur.

A woman passing by looked at the two of them. "A dog in a hospital!" she said with some disapproval.

"Tyler's part of a special program," I explained. "For people who like animals, it can be very comforting to be with one."

Taking it in, the woman paused and then said, "My son is blind and he's never been near a dog. Could you bring Tyler to him?"

"Sure," I said.

Hooked up to an IV unit, her three-year-old looked so small and helpless. When his mother took his hand he turned toward her. "Kenny," she said, "there's a friend here to visit you. His name is Tyler, and he's a big, beautiful gold-colored dog."

Approaching slowly, Tyler rested his head on the bed. When the mother guided Kenny's hand to Tyler, the boy's eyes grew wide. As he began petting the dog, his face was transformed by a giant smile. Soon he had his arms around Tyler's neck.

A couple of times a month, I took Tyler to the hospital. Beforehand I always gave him a bath. He didn't like it, but he knew it meant he would be seeing the kids soon, and when I called him, he came running. At lunchtime we would pick up a hamburger and French fries at McDonald's and share them in the car. Then we would go back to CHOP.

I had been a pediatric nurse for sixteen years, but seeing how much Tyler comforted the children gave me a new enthusiasm for my work. Other dogs joined the pet-therapy program, and the staff welcomed their visits. "They make me feel good," said one of the nurses.

Then one afternoon I was drying Tyler off after his bath, and I felt a lump on his neck. I knew better than to ignore such things, especially after battling breast cancer myself ten years earlier. I rushed him to our veterinarian. A few days later we got the results of his tests. He had cancer.

"It's in the early stages," the veterinarian said reassuringly. "You might be able to save him." He referred us to Dr. Ann Jeglum, a veterinarian who specializes in treating animals with cancer. "If he were my dog, I would do everything I could."

Wasn't that how I had treated my breast cancer? Since then I had met plenty of other people who had survived the disease. Why shouldn't my dog? God had given him a purpose in life, and I wanted to do everything in my power to help him continue in it. *Lord, you'll have to help us through this,* I prayed.

Tyler had his first dose of chemotherapy that same day. He was even taking some of the same medication I had. Throughout his treatment he was quieter and less lively than usual, though he never shied away from going to the vet. The hardest part was seeing his beautiful golden fur fall out, but Tyler didn't seem to mind looking as though he had been clipped.

During that time I couldn't take him to CHOP. I think he missed it. I know the staff and patients missed him. When I told one little girl that my dog was being treated for cancer, she asked me if he had lost his hair. "Yes," I said, "but it'll grow back."

"Will mine?" she asked, rubbing her almost bald head.

"Yes," I replied. "And it will be beautiful."

She smiled and said, "Tell your dog I said hello."

After several months the chemotherapy treatments were completed and tests indicated Tyler's cancer was in remission. "He'll still have to be tested every month," Dr. Jeglum said. "If it comes back, we'll catch it right away."

When we left her office, Tyler's tail was wagging happily.

To celebrate our good news, I took him to McDonald's on the way home, just like old times.

In a few weeks Tyler was well enough to go back to work. As I opened the car door for him, I realized he probably thought we were going for another checkup at the vet. "We're going to CHOP, Tyler!" I announced. At the hospital he bounded out of the car.

In the ICU he made his way eagerly down the hall. He was back where he wanted to be. "It's Tyler!" one of the nurses exclaimed. The children reached out to hug and pet him.

As we came out of one room, a boy in a wheelchair was waiting for us in the corridor. He knew Tyler from earlier hospital stays. This time the boy was recovering from surgery to remove a brain tumor, and his head had been shaved.

Leaning forward to pet Tyler, he said, "What happened to you? Where's your fur?"

When I told him, he took Tyler's head in both hands and kissed him. "I hope you feel better, bud—real soon!" He was doing for Tyler what Tyler had done for so many children. He was letting him know that he wasn't alone and that he was loved. That's what God put us here for, to comfort one another—dogs and humans alike.

The Mangy Angel

Esther L. Vogt

Cold March showers pelted my face as I stepped from the warmth of the church and threaded my way across the lot toward the parsonage.

Thursday evening's meeting of the women's missionary society had finally closed, and, as the pastor's wife, I was the last to leave.

My husband had gone to a general conference in Detroit, and the children and I were alone. I half expected to find the parsonage cloaked with night, for the hour was late and the children should have been in bed hours ago.

Letting myself in quietly, I was surprised to find the kitchen light still burning. Ted, our oldest, his dark head bent over his books, was studying at the table. He looked up as I came in.

"Hi, Mom. Wet out, isn't it?"

"It's a wild night, all right," I said wryly, peeling off my dripping coat and boots.

He went back to his homework.

As I turned to leave the kitchen I looked down. Then I gasped. Our huge mangy dog lay stretched out at Ted's side!

"Ted! What's Brownie doing in the house?" I demanded. "You know he's never stayed inside before!"

Ted glanced up from his book and shrugged. "Why, he just wanted in, so I let him in. Then I decided I might as well bring my homework down here."

Brownie wanted in! That, in itself, was utterly incongruous. For that matter, so was everything else about that dog.

Black, brown, and smelly—and of undetermined breed—he had wandered to the parsonage one day and simply decided to stay. He adopted our family and was fiercely protective of us in every way. In fact, he loved us so much that he wanted to be where we were. Yet once we'd let him into the house, he developed a peculiar claustrophobic streak. He would race in terror from window to door to window until we'd let him out. No amount of bribing or petting could persuade Brownie to remain indoors. Even the dreary drip-drip of rain from the eaves failed to lure him inside. He preferred the most inclement outdoor weather to being enclosed.

Until now.

There he was, lying calmly beside Ted in the kitchen like a very ordinary house dog.

I remembered his previous fierce possessiveness of us. Our large, red-brick parsonage sprawled comfortably on a big grassy plot behind the church and opposite the public school. Children often cut across the church property and through our yard when hurrying to and from school. We didn't mind. In fact, they were our friends. Against our better judgment, we often had report cards thrust at us even before parents saw them.

That is, until the dog came. He growled threateningly at

anyone who dared cross our yard. Yet Brownie always came when I called him off.

Still, with people dropping in at our parsonage at all hours of the day, I was afraid some day I wouldn't get him called off in time.

I tried desperately to find another home for him, but with no success. Once I even called the Humane Society.

"Sure, lady," they said. "We'll get him. But you gotta catch him and shut him up for us."

Shut Brownie up? Impossible! One might as well try to imprison a victim of claustrophobia in an elevator! Until a better solution presented itself, he would have to remain with us.

And that's how things stood that wild, stormy night I came home from church.

Shaking my head at Brownie's strange behavior, I went down to the basement to bolt the door that leads to the outside. I came back up directly and retired to the living room with the paper.

Ted already had gone up to bed, and I decided to turn in too. The dog still lay on the kitchen floor, his shaggy head resting on his front paws.

Better put Brownie out first, I thought as I entered the kitchen to lock the back door. Rain still drummed steadily against the windows.

But when I tried to get the dog out of the door, he refused to budge. I wheedled; I coaxed. I pushed and pulled. He remained stationary.

Going to the refrigerator, I took out a chunk of meat and

tried to bribe him to the door by dangling it in front of him. He still refused to move.

With a bewildered sigh I picked up his hind end, yanked him toward the door, and out of it. Like quicksilver, his front end slid back in!

I grabbed his front end, and the back was in. His four feet seemed like a baker's dozen. He was stubborn, determined, yet somehow placid. Talk about Balaam's donkey—I knew exactly how Balaam felt.

Should I call Ted to help me? No, the hour was late and Ted needed his sleep. I decided to shut all the doors to the kitchen and leave the dog inside. Then I went wearily to bed.

The next morning the dog reverted to his true nature and frantically tore out of the house.

A puzzled frown ribbed my forehead as I went down to the basement to turn on the furnace. What had made Brownie behave so strangely? Why had he been determined to remain in the house this one particular night? I shook my head. There seemed to be no answer.

When I reached the bottom of the stairs, I felt a breath of cold, damp air. Then a queer, slimy feeling swept over me. The outside door was open! Was someone in the basement?

After the first wave of panic had drained from me, my reasoning returned.

Someone had gone out of the basement!

Limp with the reality of that fact, I looked around. The windows were as snug and tight on the inside as ever. Whoever had gone out of that door had been in when I had gone down to bolt it the night before! He apparently had heard my unsuccessful attempts to put the dog out and knew he had to come up through the kitchen and face the dog—or go out the door he had come in earlier.

That smelly, stray pooch had known this, and God had used him to keep us safe. Why didn't he growl or bark? I don't know. Maybe he knew he didn't have to.

I had always believed that God has definite work for his holy angels, and that as his child I could lay claim to the verse in Hebrews 1:14: "Are they [angels] not all ministering spirits sent forth to minister for them who shall be heirs of salvation?"

But his "ministering spirit" had taken a peculiar form that wild, stormy night. Instead of glorious, dazzling wings, the Lord had given our guardian angel four stubborn, mangy feet!

Floodhound

Joe Mike Brooks

Our family has been living in Bevil Oaks for eleven years. It's a small town in southeast Texas that lounges along the southern edge of the Big Thicket Forest and nudges the banks of the Pine Island Bayou. We're a very close community. I wouldn't live anywhere else. There are seven of us: Susie; me; our sons, Paul and Andrew; their sister Amy; her little Maltese pup; and, of course, B.D.

B.D. is part Lab, part Walker hound and part who-knows-quite-what. In other words, he's a very big mutt. Our oldest son, Andrew, got B.D. two Christmases before, the same year Amy got her Maltese puppy. Those pups were a sight, as the tiny white Maltese ran circles around the clumsy, lumbering mongrel. We called them Little Pup and Big Dog—L.P. and B.D. for short.

Our beautiful sanctuary has its darker moments, caused by the fierce rainstorms we sometimes get. Rain isn't taken lightly around Bevil Oaks. Rain means trouble.

In all our years here we've seen the bayou break its banks many times. And when the monster is out of its cage, watch out. The water can rise swiftly. Neighbors help neighbors. Everyone pitches in, piling sandbag after sandbag in hopes of damming the flow and saving homes and businesses. Our family had always been among the lucky ones, avoiding disaster even through hurricanes.

Sunday, October 16, 1994, dawned with a misty, drizzling rain. But the drizzle turned to steady rain and then to a downpour. By Tuesday, some twenty inches had flooded the bayou basin. We'd never seen flooding like this before. Houses were being swamped; families were grabbing what they could and evacuating—and the water just kept on rising.

We worked frantically with our lower-elevation neighbors all day Wednesday, propping up furniture on sawhorses, rolling rugs where we could, and removing photo albums and mementos altogether.

By nightfall I was keyed up and wide-awake, but I knew I needed to get some rest for the next day. As I locked the front door, I peered out at our driveway. The water was high in our ditches, but had been draining steadily toward the bayou all day. Our home appeared to be safe from the flood. Just to be sure, I decided to drive a stick into the ground near the side of the house so I could keep an eye on the level of the water that was already sloshing across our yard. I yanked on my boots, and immediately B.D. was at my side. He's very protective— he circled around me as I checked the house. His doghouse out back was already full of water, so he was staying in the garage that night.

It was 11:30 P.M. when B.D. and I finished making the rounds. Andrew, Amy and Paul were asleep. Paul's girlfriend, Wendy, who had been stranded at our home by the water, was asleep in Amy's room. B.D. curled up on his blanket inside the garage. In our room, Susie lay awake. "I can't help worrying about our friends who had to leave their homes," she said. We prayed for them and our own family, and I fell asleep wondering what tomorrow would bring.

In the middle of the night the phone rang. It was Trina, the wife of our church's music minister. We had seen her earlier that day, as she and her husband, John, helped some families leave their homes. *Does another family need help?* I wondered. "Get up," Trina told Susie, "and get out! The entire city has to evacuate."

Susie hung up and tried to turn on a light, but our power was off. I fumbled with my boots and hurried outside to check my stick. B.D. followed as I waded into the yard. Only a nub of stick was visible. The water had risen a good ten inches in three hours.

I waded out toward the street and looked around. There was silence. The familiar forest noises of insects and critters were gone. The stars were hidden behind low clouds and a soft mist floated around me in the darkness. Nothing stirred except B.D. and me. It was then that I beheld the strangest sight I've ever seen: the water was flowing backward up the drainage ditches! It was like the whole earth had shifted. Our driveway was submerged and the houses down the street looked like dim islands. I ran back inside, B.D. splashing at my heels.

"Let's pack the Cherokee and hit the road," I said to Susie. I could tell she was scared.

"I guess that's best," she said quietly. "But where will we go?"

"We'll stay at my office in Beaumont." I lit some candles on the dresser. "The sooner we leave, the better."

I woke the kids and tried to get everybody organized, while Susie grabbed blankets, filled suitcases, and packed coolers. We worked with quiet urgency in a house lit only by candles and flashlights. The kids loaded the Jeep to the ceiling and we were set to go. Amy, Paul, Andrew, and Wendy piled in the back seat, our Maltese jumped in Amy's lap, and Susie, arms full of groceries, hopped in the front.

Then there was B.D.

B.D. just watched us from the porch, not moving a hair, tail held high. He seemed to want to stand his ground against the rising water. I knew that dog well enough to understand there was no way of making him do what he didn't want to. Besides, if any dog could survive a flood, it would be a big, strong swimmer like B.D.

"Hang on, everybody," I said. I ran back into the garage, put a bucket full of dog food on a workbench and left the garage door partly open. *At least B.D. will have shelter and food until we come back,* I thought, consoling myself as I climbed back in the Jeep.

I slipped the Jeep into gear and focused my attention on getting us to dry land. *Lord, please lead us out of here safely,* I prayed.

I pulled out into the flooded street, turning slowly. Then I saw a flash of yellow fur in my side mirror. It couldn't be, but it was: B.D.! He bounded through the water behind us and ran up alongside the Jeep. Despite all our yelling for him to go back, he kept near us for the next two blocks. Then the water got deep.

The darkness of the water and the night sky blended. Squinting through the rain-spattered windshield, I could just barely make out the tops of the mailboxes lining the street. I used them as guideposts. My five passengers had quieted down. We scarcely breathed. Each of us knew that one wrong move could land us in a ditch, and most certainly underwater.

Suddenly B.D. paddled out ahead of us. He seemed to know exactly where we were going. Forging ahead, he somehow stayed on the highest ground, blazing a course for us down the middle of the streets. Sometimes the water lapped B.D.'s ankles; sometimes he was swimming. But our big yellow dog didn't relent. If he got too far ahead of us, he'd wait for our Jeep to catch up.

The foggy rain blurred the windshield. I fought hard to hold my concentration. The most dangerous parts were the turns at intersections, with drainage ditches on all sides. Turning too sharply or too widely could land the Jeep in six feet of water. But somehow B.D. knew precisely how to guide me into a perfect turn. Once, when I tried to go my own way instead of following his lead, we got stuck in the mud on top of the median.

B.D. led us two miles to the highway and another mile toward town, past stranded cars, flooded yards and water up to the windows on most of the homes in Bevil Oaks. Across a distance that normally takes ten minutes, B.D. guided us fearlessly for an hour and a half.

When the highway emerged from the floodwaters, we pulled over and opened the door. There he was, panting and tired, his tongue flopped to one side. B.D. jumped in unprompted. That big, wet, smelly dog sat right on Susie's lap, accepting hugs and praise from everyone.

We know now that Big Dog is not a mixed-breed mutt after all. He's a full-blooded, pedigreed Floodhound. The only one we know in all of Texas.

You can never tell where help is going to come from. One day we're helping our neighbors, and the next our family dog is helping us. B.D. led us safely through the deadly floodwaters that night, but I know who was leading B.D. Through all our journeys, God serves as our guide. He sends his angels in a variety of forms to help. It just so happens that ours has a tail.

Jocko—
at Your Service

Marilyn Mesi Pona

I will never forget what it was like to be disabled—and to need a helpful companion at my side.

Some time back I suffered through six years of intense back pain. Scoliosis had deformed my right hip and put me first on crutches, then in a wheelchair. I'd always been an active person, and losing my mobility was frustrating. I was constantly dropping socks and pens and utensils that were impossible for me to pick up. My life was strewn with objects I couldn't reach, doors I couldn't maneuver through, and tiny chores I couldn't manage. My husband and three children helped me as much as possible, but they couldn't be with me all the time.

At last, doctors operated and removed pieces of ruptured disks that had twisted a nerve in my spine. The excruciating pain was gone. I could walk again! I went home, thanking God for my recovery.

But the energy I had mustered to fight the pain swirled inside me with no place to go. My children were growing up and busy with activities of their own; my husband had his job. Now what would fill my time?

I tried gardening, joined clubs, volunteered at animal shelters, and took walks with my Labrador retriever, Max. But nothing challenged me. I couldn't help feeling there was some project that I was meant to do. I'd prayed for help during my time of pain, and I prayed now for guidance.

And then a news item about Sandy Maze of Columbus, Ohio, appeared on television. Sandy, who had muscular dystrophy, had paid a trainer to teach her dog, Stormy, to help her with simple but important tasks, such as retrieving keys, pencils and other objects. With Stormy's help, Sandy had been able to get around on her own, to lead a fuller, richer life, and even to attend college. The experiment had worked so well that Sandy had started a group called Support Dogs for the Handicapped so that others could benefit from having a dog like hers.

I was thrilled! Here were the "friends" that could give an invaluable helping hand—or paw—to handicapped or disabled people. And here was the challenge I had been looking for. I picked up the phone and called Sandy. I'd start a group of my own in St. Louis!

With Sandy's long-distance encouragement and advice, I actually was able to train Max to pick up objects, to prop open doors, to carry the phone receiver to and from its cradle, and to help me get in and out of my wheelchair.

Soon I was speaking to local groups and organizations, explaining how useful support dogs could be. If I could arouse interest and raise money for a nonprofit organization in the St. Louis area, then I could educate others and help train dogs for handicapped people who might not otherwise know about or be able to afford training a dog on their own.

People listened sympathetically—but found it hard to understand how such a program would work in a practical way. My words weren't enough. I needed a dog right up there with me to demonstrate.

I tried to use Max. But Max didn't like crowds and would freeze or retreat into the wings.

I had to have another dog. I talked to breeders, went to dog shows, and answered ads in the paper. I saw sleek dogs, fuzzy dogs, well-bred dogs, frisky dogs—all handsome and well-groomed. But they were too high-strung, or too skittery, or too lackadaisical. Not one animal I "interviewed" seemed right. But somehow I sensed that God had a dog waiting for me out there—a special dog.

And then one day while I was visiting the Open Door Animal Sanctuary in House Springs, about twenty miles from my home, I passed the pen where puppies were kept.

And there sitting stoically among the bouncing, rollicking pups, was a huge mound of a grown-up dog, with large, dark eyes and a penetrating gaze.

At first I almost laughed out loud. On my second look, I almost wept. I can't remember seeing a more road-worn, tattered animal. The dog was scarred and bruised, but his big brown eyes seemed to be telling me something.

"What are you doing here with the puppies?" I asked. His tail gave a thump. As I walked away, I knew he was watching me.

"That's Jocko," the girl in the office told me. "Or at least that's what we're calling him." He'd been found wandering on the highway. He was part Great Dane, part retriever, around four years old, and had probably been abused. "We had to put him in with the puppies," the girl explained, "because he kept jumping our fences, and the puppies' pen is the only one that's covered."

I walked back to the pen. On closer inspection, poor Jocko looked not better, but worse. An infection had eaten away part of one ear. And when, with an apologetic air, he leaned back to scratch, I saw that his paw pads were raw.

He was a mess. Who would ever think of adopting such a dog? God would. *Look beyond the outward appearance*, a voice inside me whispered. *This dog is special. This is the one you've been looking for.*

I took Jocko for a "test run," walking along the road. He wasn't spooked by roaring cars or sudden noises or new people, and he seemed alert and easygoing.

When I took him home, the rest of the family was aghast.

"That's the new dog?"

"Gosh, he's a mess."

"Support dog? He doesn't look like he could support himself."

And then my husband drove up, took one look out the car window, and drove off in mock horror. After circling the block, he returned and got out to gape. "You've got to be kidding," he said.

But Jocko didn't seem at all concerned that he wasn't getting the "Beautiful Pet of the Year" award. He wagged his tail, and by the next day all I heard was, "We're keeping that nice dog, aren't we?"

I scrubbed him up, gave him his medicine, and just two days later took him to a muscular dystrophy camp. Jocko quickly became the center of attention, and loved it. He didn't cringe or snap when eager-but-uncoordinated hands reached out to pet or hug him. And if it was awkward for a person in a wheelchair to reach him, he would maneuver his head under that hand. Ah, this was the temperament I had been searching for.

Now how would he take to training? Well, he didn't have to be taught to be a ham. On Halloween he went trick-or-treating, carrying a purse in his mouth and acting as if he had done it all his life.

But what about the specifics and disciplines of training? I started by teaching him simple commands like "come," "stay," "heel," "sit" and "stand," using both voice and hand signals. I helped things along by hooking Jocko's leash to Max's collar; when Max performed his own retrieval tasks, Jocko was pulled right along.

The weeks went by. Jocko had to be trained not just to pick up an object, but also to hold on until a hand was ready to take it. Picking up a telephone receiver was one thing—but if the receiver was dropped halfway across the room, it didn't do a handicapped person much good. Over and over and over again I worked with Jocko, sometimes assisted by Max, until Jocko got the point: Pick up an object and carry it to the waiting person's hand.

Nine months passed, and Jocko's appearance underwent a startling transformation. His emaciated frame filled out, and his coat started to shine. His once-infected cauliflower ear was still scrunched in, but now he stood tall and had a spring in his step.

Jocko was ready for his first demonstration. I took him before a group of rambunctious second-graders. As Jocko retrieved a pencil, an eraser, and assorted other objects, the youngsters watched with rapt attention. And they burst into applause when Jocko helped me out of a chair by pulling me up as I hung on to his leash. Jocko's performance was flawless; I said a silent prayer of thanks. This was the special dog God had intended for me.

Soon Jocko and I were doing two to four demonstrations a week. He would pick up my cane, my keys—even a dime. He would help me up steps, or stand still and firm so that I could show how someone who had fallen could use a dog as a brace to get up.

By now people were asking for "the lady with the big yellow dog." Jocko had become a pro, ready and willing to be petted, talked to, and photographed.

Over the following months, more and more people were able to see how helpful—even essential—a dog could be to a handicapped person.

Bit by bit, people offered money, time, skills, and services. In May 1983, Support Dogs for the Handicapped was officially incorporated in St. Louis as a nonprofit organization. And Jocko's stardom continued to grow when he was nominated as Service Dog of the Year. But in spite of his new-found fame, he still kept all four feet on the ground: Whenever I had a relapse and my back acted up again, Jocko still acted as my support dog. He literally gave me a boost and eased my way.

Again and again Jocko rose to the occasion. And because of him, a whole new battalion of dogs and puppies are doing the same. Today, in addition to the adult dogs that our group trains, we also breed the most suitable dogs and will start training puppies at the earliest possible age.

I think back to eight years ago—to a raggedy old pooch and a frustrated former invalid, both needing something to do. And I thank God, who got us together and turned us into a golden dog and an active lady, eager to let you know that, no matter how bent over or beat up you are, you too can rise to the occasion—and have the full, rich life God intends you to have.

You can bet a pen full of puppies on it.

The Three of Us

Edda Christine Drey

S mokey was Pete's dog. From the first days when she came to us as a pup, this Australian blue heeler followed my husband all over our small Iowa farm, trotting happily at his heels while he fed the stock, repaired the machinery, and tended the crops. While Pete waved and yelled, Smokey nipped at the heels of our cows and pigs, sorting them out and herding them back to their proper stalls in the barn.

Smokey had Pete's schedule down so exactly that if Pete took a little longer than Smokey thought necessary, she'd bark at him to hurry up. And at night, while we watched television, Smokey would flop at the side of Pete's chair. Granted, every now and then Smokey would come to take a sniff at what I was up to, but basically that dog made it clear that her world revolved around Pete.

Or so I thought until one unforgettable Tuesday.

On the morning of November 5, 1985, Pete and Smokey set off across the yard, together as usual. Today we would be hauling in the corn.

Pete went out on the tractor to do the harvesting. I bumped along behind him on our old Farmall H tractor, transporting the loads of corn back to the building site beside the hog and cattle yards, where I unloaded them all into the "elevator" that clickety-clacked its way up into the corn crib.

I had already collected two wagonloads from Pete and was unloading the third, when I realized that some of the ears of corn had spilled onto the ground. As I bent down alongside the moving elevator to pick up the wayward ears, my foot slipped into a rut made by the tractor wheel after a recent rain.

I was trying to regain my balance when I felt a hard tug on my pant leg. *What's that?* I wondered. In a split second I knew.

I screamed in horror and pain.

My coveralls had been caught in the churning power takeoff that drove the elevator. Within seconds my entire leg had been wound in too.

Somehow I was able to throw myself against the machinery's motor and shut it off. My head and shoulders hit the ground with a thud.

I inched myself up on my elbows and stared in disbelief at the sight of my foot and leg mangled in the machinery. Waves of nausea swept through me. *I mustn't lose consciousness,* I told myself. *I might never wake up.*

I sank back down and closed my eyes, too sickened to think clearly. In the distance I heard Pete's tractor making its rounds in the fields; my cries would never be heard over the roar. How long would it take before Pete realized something was wrong?

A shadow fell across my face. Smokey. She was standing over me whimpering.

"Go get Pete," I ordered her. "Smokey, go get Pete."

She looked as though she understood what I was saying. She walked a few feet away and started to bark in the direction of the field, then turned and came right back.

I repeated the command. "Go get Pete!"

Again Smokey went a little way and barked in Pete's direction. But she would not go out into the field and get him. Instead she came back to where I was lying and placed her head on my shoulder.

The noise of Pete's tractor came closer. I reached for my cap that had tumbled off, raised my arm as high as I could, and waved and waved. But the grass around me was too high. The tractor roared off in the opposite direction.

"Go get Pete!" I pleaded once again to Smokey, and again she got up, went a few feet, barked, and then returned to lie beside me.

I squinted up into the sun. How could this have happened to me? Where was God? Where was God when my foot slipped?

Pete doesn't know why he came to check on me. I'd been helping him with the corn for over thirty years, so there was no reason for him to think that I'd need his help. But "for some strange reason" (which is how he put it later) he stopped his tractor and came to see how I was doing.

He found me, still conscious, with Smokey's head on my shoulder.

The following weeks in the hospital were hard. My leg had to be amputated just above the knee. And I had to start

readjusting to a new life, with only one leg. Before the accident I'd thought my faith in God had been pretty strong, but
now I had to confess there were moments I felt abandoned.
Where was God when my foot slipped into that rut?

Doctors fitted me with an artificial leg that I strapped
around my waist. Getting used to it wasn't easy, but finally I
was ready to return home. A bed was set up for me in the
downstairs dining room, where I could sit by the window and
look out at the neighboring farms. My husband, children, and
friends were there continually to comfort and help me in all
my waking hours. But there were still periods of time when I
was—and felt—very alone. What would I do when my family
and friends had to get back to their daily routines? Would I be
left all alone?

But guess who never left my side. Smokey.

I'd never seen such a change in an animal. Smokey
parked herself by my bed and stayed there. At night I'd wake
up and there she'd be, her head on the covers looking straight
at me. She wouldn't even leave the room to eat; she lost
weight and started getting weak, so someone had to bring food
in to her!

When visitors came and I'd start to get tired, Smokey
would put herself between me and them and bare her teeth.
She seemed to know exactly how I was feeling at any given
moment. And no matter how much activity there was around
my bed, she never got underfoot. Although she was known for
being pretty lively, she never raced around or got agitated.
Pete was afraid she might trip me when I got up. But when-

ever I tried to walk by myself, using crutches and balancing on my new leg, Smokey moved out of the way. One day I fell, and she ran to the door and barked furiously until Pete came to help me up.

"That dog has set herself up as your guardian angel," Pete said one night after doing the evening chores.

"Some guardian angel!" I sputtered. "Why wouldn't she help me the day of the accident?"

"I think she helped more than you're willing to admit," Pete said on his way to the shower. "She stood by you."

Stood by me.

I stirred uncomfortably on the bed, and Smokey sat up and put her face on the covers. For the first time since coming back from the hospital, I really looked at her. There was no mistaking it: In her eyes was a concern that I had been too preoccupied and upset to notice before.

Smokey rested her head on the top of my bed, and I let the love from those eyes flow through me. I almost felt that if she could talk she would have said, "Chris, I love you and care about you. Every minute that you were out there suffering, I was suffering with you."

Then suddenly it was as if God himself were speaking to me. It wasn't God's fault that I'd been in too much of a hurry to shut off the machinery motor before bending down close to it. The accident was just that, an accident. Now, through Smokey's eyes, I felt that God was trying to say he too had suffered along with me during those agonizing first hours, and throughout the recovery time that followed. They'd both stood by me.

I reached out and rubbed Smokey behind the ears, and her tail began to thump against the covers.

From that point on, my recovery progressed so well that soon I was ready for another leg. It looks so real that I feel comfortable wearing dresses again. These days I drive the car or pickup by myself. I work regularly at the school library and continue to be active in our church. I do all my own housework, and I still help out as much as possible with the farm chores, but I'm mighty careful whenever I'm around any equipment.

Smokey and I are still close friends. She leaves me now from time to time, but checks with me first. I have to tell her, "You go ahead. I'll be fine." Then she follows Pete across the yard as he goes to do the chores, always looking back to make sure I'm really okay.

Smokey, our Australian blue heeler. Heeler . . . healer? Maybe to some people it's a strange play on words. But somehow I'm sure God used that Australian blue heeler to heal me.

Family Hero

Pam Sica

How old is Bullet now?" the vet asked as he lifted our old golden retriever up on the examination table. "Thirteen," I said. He put his stethoscope on Bullet's shaggy chest and leaned forward. "I don't like what I'm hearing," he said. "I'll have to do an electrocardiogram."

The EKG led to a blood test, which led to the discovery of a growth on his liver. The vet's prognosis was grim: If we didn't operate soon, Bullet would die. The cost of the operation, including sonograms, x-rays, blood work and medicine would be costly. "I know how much Bullet means to you," the vet said, "but the average life span of a golden retriever is ten to thirteen years. Why don't you go home and think about what you want to do?"

On the way home I stopped by the grocery store where I bumped into a neighbor and explained my dilemma. "Pam," she said, "the dog is thirteen years old. He's had a good life. Let him go."

"I can't. Bullet is family. We've been through everything together."

He had arrived at my doorstep in a wicker basket wearing a red bow—a gift from my husband to save our faltering marriage. Bullet had shiny brown eyes and thumped his tail. The marriage did not work, but Bullet stayed. On nights when I returned home late from my restaurant job, Bullet would nuzzle me and rest his chin reassuringly on my lap.

By the time I was ready to start dating again, he became my best chaperon. If he didn't like a guy, his tail drooped and he refused to be petted. For those lucky ones who passed muster, he'd wag his tail, fetch his favorite chewed-up ground-hog toy, deposit it at the guy's feet, then look over at me as if to say, "This one might be okay."

Several years later, a new part-time security guard named Troy started working at the hotel restaurant where I worked. One snowy night near closing time, one of the gals and I were having some hot chocolate. Troy waltzed in, covered with snow. "Looks good," he said. "Could you make me some?"

Something about his attitude made me snap back, "Kitchen's over there. Make it yourself."

My friend chided me for being rude, but I was unrepentant. Out in the parking lot the snow was piled in three-foot drifts. I scraped it off my Oldsmobile Cutlass, got in and turned the key. Nothing doing. I tried again and again, my fingers near freezing. Feeling pretty sheepish, I headed back to the hotel to find our new security guard.

"I think my battery is dead," I told him. "Do you have some jumper cables?"

Troy's brown eyes danced, and he could barely suppress a grin. "Do you mean you want me to help you?"

My Cutlass refused to start and Troy had to give me a lift

home. No sooner had he dropped me off than he was ringing my doorbell. His truck was stuck at the end of my driveway, and he had to sleep on my couch, with Bullet standing guard.

The next morning he shoveled my front walk and driveway, got his truck running, and drove to the convenience store around the corner. He returned with steaming coffee, orange juice, and doughnuts. We sat around the kitchen table. Bullet wagged his tail and licked Troy's hand. He brought his old stuffed groundhog toy and dropped it in Troy's lap. Bullet didn't want this one to get away. Neither did I.

All the happiness that I had missed in my first marriage I found with Troy. He was funny, kind, and as much a dog lover as I was. We looked forward to raising a family. Unfortunately, whenever I conceived I couldn't carry a baby past two months.

"That's all right," we told each other. "We have Bullet." We took him to the park, to Florida, to the beach—all those places you go with a kid. We bought Christmas presents for him and celebrated his birthdays.

That's why it was devastating to contemplate his loss. "The vet says that the tests and the operation will cost a fortune," I told Troy after Bullet's exam. "But I don't see any other choice. Bullet helped me when I was at my lowest. Now I need to help him."

Before the surgery we took Bullet to our parish priests. Father Mike and Pastor Ryan said a prayer and blessed him. I prayed, *Dear God, if you still have some purpose for him, don't take Bullet from us. Not yet. Please.*

The surgery was a success. Bullet came home, and in a

matter of weeks he was his old self again. Of course, he moved a little slower and wasn't as fast at fetching his chew toy, but then I didn't run after him as quickly as I used to. He might have been thirteen, but I was forty.

That summer I experienced some recurring nausea I wrote off as indigestion. Troy talked me into taking an over-the-counter pregnancy test. The test was positive! We hugged and laughed and cried, while Bullet ran around us carrying the empty pregnancy-test box in his mouth like a trophy.

Troy Joseph was born on April 10, 2002. We'd done all we could to prepare Bullet for the addition to the family, showing him the crib and the changing table and the baby clothes we'd been given. The nurse on the maternity ward suggested getting him accustomed to the smell of the baby. "Take your dog one of little Troy's blankets so he can get used to his scent."

Later that night Troy called me at the hospital from home. "You're not going to believe this. I gave Bullet the blanket and he won't let go of it. Right now he's all curled up sleeping with it."

We brought Troy home and set him in his car seat on the living-room floor. Bullet came over to investigate. He looked, sniffed, and wagged his tail. No matter where I took the baby, Bullet was by our side. Even at night, instead of sleeping at the foot of our bed, Bullet curled up next to the crib. Little Troy was his.

On the morning of May 1, we were awakened at four

o'clock by Troy's alarm. He was going back to work for the first time since the baby was born.

"You get ready," I told him. "I'll take care of the baby."

I changed Troy Joseph's diaper and put him on our bed. Bullet stayed in our bedroom while I went to the kitchen to warm a bottle. I was standing at the kitchen sink, testing the milk on my wrist, when Bullet came barreling down the hall, jumping and barking furiously.

"Want to go out?" I asked. I opened the door, but he wouldn't budge. He stared at me with pleading eyes, barked, then tore back down the hallway. *Crazy dog!* I followed, stopping at the bathroom to ask Troy to test the temperature of the milk. Bullet returned, barking with a vengeance.

"What's the matter with him?" Troy asked.

"I don't know. He doesn't want to go out."

In our bedroom Bullet sat whimpering by our bed. By the glow of the night-light I could see the baby's head thrown back in an odd way. He was making faint gurgling noises. I picked him up and watched in horror as he went from purple to blue, then grew limp in my arms.

"Troy!" I screamed and dashed to dial 911. "The baby's stopped breathing!" Troy tried to do CPR until the police and EMTs arrived. Bullet followed them in, barking frantically. I had to drag him into the kitchen and barricade the door with two chairs so he couldn't get out.

The EMTs managed to resuscitate our baby before they whisked him off in the ambulance. His father rode with him, and I followed in the truck. For the next sixteen days Troy

Joseph stayed in the pediatric intensive care unit. After countless tests, it was determined that his breathing problem was caused by double pneumonia and undiagnosed heart irregularities.

"You're lucky you found your baby when you did," said the doctor. "Had any more time passed, he most likely would not have survived."

Troy Joseph is doing fine now. We monitor his situation with frequent doctor visits. As for Bullet, I thank God for every day that he's still around. He's more than a hero in our house. He's an answer to prayer.

Love Finds
the Way

Gail Turnmire

From the moment we spotted Cody at the animal shelter, we knew he was our new dog. He locked eyes with my husband John and never diverted his gaze, never blinked. Those shiny brown eyes and that big, goofy grin won us over in a heartbeat.

Cody is a mix of golden retriever, Siberian husky, collie, and yellow Labrador retriever—with all four breeds' voices. He howls, sings, barks, chatters, and can be quiet when it's appropriate. At first glance, he has a golden's coat, but with a ring of thick, white, cotton-candy fur around his neck, from the collie. He walked well out in front when we hiked—no heeling here. And, many a summer's day would find Cody proudly prancing around the yard, fluffy tail spinning like a rudder, with a "prize" in his mouth. The prize was never chewed or bitten, but laid inside his mouth, held tight by that loose retriever lip skin made to carry home the bird.

Years later, a move to New Mexico meant the dog that used to curl up on top of the picnic table to savor snowy winter blizzards would have to adjust to sunshine and wind. He did. Cody scoped out the small patch of dirt that ran between the hedge and sidewalk along the front of the house. It was shady somewhere along that span all day. He raked away the leaves, dug out a few dozen freshly planted flowers, scraped the surface until he had a comfortable dirt doggie bed, and planted himself. From this vantage point, he could watch the road, the driveway, the mailbox, and the neighbor's horses and dogs.

But hiking manners and guard duties aside, Cody's heart is what makes him special. When John became ill, Cody stood in front of him, across his legs, as the visiting nurse examined him. He smiled sweetly, but was in the way, nonetheless. He didn't stop grinning, but he didn't move, either. The nurse got used to leaning over Cody to reach John.

When John died, Cody spent three days outside, lying in the same spot, waiting. With paws crossed and an alert, on-duty expression on his face, he waited for the red '53 pickup truck to come home. No amount of coaxing could bring him in, even at night. He ate little and drank only enough water. His attention couldn't be diverted—he wouldn't give up. When he finally did come inside, he didn't leave my side for seven days, except for short potty trips outside.

Today, at age fourteen, after having cruciate ligament surgery, Cody still works his property several times a day. His big heart and overwhelming compassion for people who need him, however, has no boundaries.

Recently our neighbor died. When I left for work that morning, I closed my gate but forgot to lock it. As our beloved neighbor was being taken away, a gust of wind blew my gate open, and Cody waddled his way next door. Rhonda, left with the sound of slamming van doors ringing in her ears, walked through her now-silent house and out the back door; the horses needed to be fed. On her patio she met Cody. He was calm and grinning, his tail spinning.

"Cody?" Rhonda asked in surprise. "Cody! What in the world are you doing here?" In her grief, she wasn't sure if she was actually seeing him. He was always in his own yard, on the other side of the fence, and he never got out. She petted him; he was the real Cody. He smiled, tongue hanging out. Together they walked out to the horse barn, Cody leaning tightly against Rhonda's leg. She clipped a lead to his collar, and they lumbered back to Cody's own yard. At the gate, Rhonda snapped off the lead. Cody walked in, and Rhonda closed the gate tightly behind him.

Cody had heard the van doors slam shut too. With less-than-perfect eyesight and having never been in Rhonda's yard, Cody found his way to her. He didn't want her to be alone. Cody knew Rhonda needed him, so he went, with the help of a gust of wind. Or so we think.

Few dogs will ever possess the depth of compassion and understanding Cody has. He truly is an angel.

Dakota's Gift

*Mike Lingenfelter
and David Frei*

L eave me alone!" I shouted to the small group that had gathered around me as I sprawled on the floor.

"Are you okay?" asked a female customer. "What can we do?"

My mind was racing: *Where am I? What am I doing here?* I'd already shoved a couple of nitroglycerin pills into my mouth, and I tried to speak more calmly to the concerned onlookers. "Just leave me alone—give my medication a chance to work." I was having a severe angina attack, and it was just my luck that I happened to be in a very public place—the local Wal-Mart. Usually Nancy helped me with the driving and kept an eye on me when I went out in public. This time, I was just trying to run a quick errand, and I hadn't given much thought to any possible heart episodes. So here I was, alone and having to worry about how everyone around me might over- or underreact, either of which could cause me problems. I was so happy with the way things were going with Dakota and my return to public life that I sometimes overlooked the fact that I was still burdened with the possibility of a health crisis at any time.

90

This was one of those times.

The heart is pretty independent and does just about anything it wants to do, good or bad. The good comes in the form of a long, healthy life. The bad is every time someone "just drops dead" from a heart attack. Now, I have unstable angina, which isn't a heart attack—but they both start out the same way, and no matter what they call it, it still hurts . . . a lot. And it scares me—I live in fear every day that my next attack will be "the big one."

Meanwhile, back at Wal-Mart, I survived, and most of the customers went back to their shopping. I unwound from the fetal position, took a few deep breaths, and sat up.

The store manager kneeled in front of me. "What do you need?" he asked. "Can we call someone?"

"I think I'll be okay in just a few more minutes. Sorry for creating a scene."

"That's the least of our concerns. I'm just glad that you're okay," he said. "I gather that you're used to dealing with this."

"Yes, I'm sorry to say I am." What I didn't share with him was that I was also feeling sorry for myself—for my vulnerability, for my loss of independence, and for the embarrassment I caused myself. Dakota was doing his job as a therapy dog, and my mental health was making a comeback—but a physical event like this one undid a lot of that psychological healing. It made me think about the fact that my life would never really get back to normal.

Being reminded of how close to death I was at any given

moment could be really depressing and scary. I couldn't escape that fear. After all, I still couldn't work, and I continued to have these attacks once or twice a week, often in an embarrassingly public way. Nancy and Jan saw to it that I stayed busy with Dakota and our animal-assisted therapy visits for Paws for Caring. That's what helped me fight back against the depression that, unfortunately, will always be there for me.

Working with kids was still the best prescription for my own well-being. There was a home and school for children with Down syndrome down the road from us. The kids went there for schooling and physical activities, ranging from walking to playing softball. "Cody," as I nicknamed him, and I made this into a family event, with Nancy and Abbey, our other golden retriever, joining us once a week throughout the summer. The children loved the dogs, and they helped motivate the kids to do a lot of different activities. It was great fun for Dakota and Abbey too—after all, who plays ball better than a golden retriever?

I was still battling angina attacks. They could happen two or three times a day, or just once or twice a week. The doctors were trying to find the right drugs and the right dosages to help me control it; and over the first eighteen months we were together, Cody witnessed hundreds of these painful episodes. He learned to crawl into bed with me or lie next to me on the floor, sometimes staying there for hours to help me fight through the attack. As my chest tied into a knot, I would squeeze him hard to shift my own pain. I know that he felt my pain, but he never flinched. There was nothing either of us could do, however, to keep these episodes from occurring.

One day in the fall of 1996, Dakota and I were visiting a school as part of Pet Awareness Week. Our veterinarian, Dr. Pat Choyce, had asked me to speak about animal-assisted therapy and service dogs. We were just starting our presentation when Cody started to act a little rambunctious. He was pawing at me and ignoring my instructions, acting as if he had a serious problem. I thought that maybe he was going to throw up or he needed to relieve himself. He'd never acted like this in public before, and, at the very least, I wanted to get him out of there to straighten him out. I was a little upset with him for making us leave in the middle of the program, but I apologized to our panel leader and took him off the stage.

I walked out the door of the auditorium; and just as the door closed behind me, I felt a crushing, sharp pain in my chest and a shortness of breath. My knees buckled and I blacked out. When I came to, there were a lot of people around me, yelling and screaming. I took my medication and sat there for a while, collecting myself as the medication went to work. Dakota, who had never left my side, was licking my arms and my face.

Dr. Choyce was there too, watching this amazing animal work on me. "Maybe he was trying to tell you something," he said.

"You may have something there," I told him.

I looked at Cody. His eyes seemed to be bluish gray, a color I'd never seen before. A few minutes later, they were back to their normal brown. I decided that I was probably seeing this color change because I was still a little out of it.

Dr. Choyce drove me home, and we talked about this episode on the way. As I looked back over the past month or so, I could remember Dakota acting the same toward me each time I had an attack. At the time, however, I was blaming him for causing them. Maybe I should have been paying closer attention to him. I talked to Nancy about it when I got home, and she pointed out that just a couple of days before, Cody had pawed at me and had gotten very agitated while I was lying on the couch. I told him to leave me alone, but he wouldn't let up. Minutes later, I had an attack. In my mind, I blamed him for making me mad enough to push me into a medical emergency.

Now, I like to think that I'm a pretty smart person: I'm an engineer, I'm well educated, and I hold something like seventeen patents. Yet I was reluctant to give Dakota credit for this ability, because I just didn't think it was possible. But in my heart (so to speak), it slowly dawned on me that somehow Dakota was sensing when these attacks were about to occur.

I was at home the next time Cody exhibited this behavior. I was sitting at my desk, working at the computer, while he napped on the carpet. Suddenly, he transformed from a well-behaved, docile golden retriever into a crazed medical caregiver. Catching me completely by surprise, he nuzzled me and pushed his head up under my arm and into my leg. I got a little perturbed as he made me spill my cup of coffee all over my desk. Since I was now paying more attention to the coffee than to him, he pawed at me, put his paw first on my arm and then my leg, and gave me a little push, as if to say, "Hey! I'm not kidding!"

Finally, I realized what he was trying to tell me. Cody was trying to save my life. I could die in the next few minutes—the coffee could wait. If I was right about Dakota, if somehow he'd learned to sense when I was about to have an angina attack, then I figured that I ought to be able to do something with that warning. I took him seriously and I swallowed my medication immediately. And sure enough, an angina attack followed. Since I felt this one coming quickly, I headed directly for my bed.

Cody didn't relax, which led me to believe that this attack was going to be a bad one. I began to get hot and started to sweat. I felt short of breath, and my heart was trying to pound its way out of my chest. I was helpless. I tried to cry out for Nancy, but I wasn't sure where she was, and Dakota wouldn't leave my side to go get her.

Clearly I wasn't in control—this dog was. He completely took charge, climbing up on my bed and looking me in the eye to reassure me that he was here. Then he turned one of those dog circles and lay down in front of me, putting his back against my chest, as if to say, *Here you go, hang on*. I gave him a quick hug and said a little prayer: "Please God, let this one be short."

God had other plans. The pain suddenly crushed me, shooting through my entire body and twisting my chest into a knot. This was a feeling I'd come to know. Normally, when an attack struck me without any warning, it would knock me to the ground. But this time, thanks to Dakota, I was ready to deal with it. Even with that advance warning, the pain quickly drained my strength, and I had to work hard to concentrate so that the medication would take effect quickly.

I felt Cody's warm body against mine, and I grabbed hold of him. In spite of the growing pain and my increasing heart rate, I sensed his steady breathing. By emulating his calm presence and synchronizing my breathing with his, I was able to control my respiration rate and keep from hyperventilating. But the pain got worse, and my bear-hugging pressure on Dakota increased. He seemed to understand; and, as he had many times before, he stayed with me without showing any sign of the pain that I know I was causing him. The time passed, and my anguish became more bearable. Little by little, the weight was lifted from my chest, I could breathe without pain, and my heart rate returned to something resembling normal.

Throughout this entire ordeal, Cody didn't move or even make a sound. As my grip on him lessened, he turned and sympathetically began to lick my hands, arms, and face. This told me that I'd survived. I rested for a few hours to regain my strength. Some of my attacks can be more serious than others, but having a warning clearly helped. The episode was much less severe than usual, and a head start on my medication helped counteract the attack, lessen its effects, and avert an accident or a fall.

How did Cody know? He was exhibiting classic "alerting" behavior, typical of seizure-alert dogs—pawing at, nuzzling, or jumping on the ill person. Some service dogs have been doing this for years, alerting their human partners about an imminent medical event, such as an epileptic seizure or diabetic emergency. I'd heard about this from some other people with service dogs—they told amazing stories of how their dogs would "alert on" them in a crisis. So I understood the principles and knew the terminology, but in all of my reading and work with doctors and service-dog owners, I hadn't heard or read about a dog alerting on someone with heart problems.

Questions filled my mind: What did Cody smell, sense, or hear? What was he thinking? How did he come to learn this behavior? What was it that finally got him to recognize what was happening to me? How did he make the leap to realizing that he could help me? And most important—did he *know* that he was saving my life? Because that's exactly what he was doing by helping me get the medication into my system in advance, just like all those seizure-alert dogs did with their people. And the support he was giving me by absorbing my crushing hugs and helping me breathe was a very big part of it as well.

On this day, Dakota gave me my freedom back.

I'd been living—and nearly dying—with these angina

attacks for close to five years. I thought back on that time frame, and about all of those scary, unpredictable episodes I'd had, such as the one in Wal-Mart. I was vulnerable and dependent on other people to help me live my life, and I had to be careful about going out in public. But maybe I could begin to look at things differently.

Now that I knew what to look for, I almost wanted to have another attack soon so I could test this theory and see if Dakota would respond the same way again. You know what they say about being careful what you wish for: Two days later I was sitting in my recliner reading the paper when that big, red, furry paw came crashing through the sports page.

"Cody!" I snapped.

He took another swipe at me with that same paw. I didn't need to be told again. I took my pills and headed for the bedroom, literally hoping that I was about to have another attack. And I did. I had this very strange mix of pain and elation—I was hurting physically, of course, but it didn't seem quite as bad as it usually did. The medication was already at work. But something else was going on. I now had an alarm system for these attacks. A four-legged, ninety-eight-pound, reddish-gold alarm system. He was taking the job away from Nancy and others. Our lives were changing once again, thanks to Dakota. . . .

Was I getting right back on the road that had led me so close to death before? Of course, working felt good to me. . . . but it also felt pretty good back in 1992. I was feeling the need to make this work, to forsake everything else in my life for success on the job.

I wanted to believe that Dakota was here to help me stay off the workaholic road. But yet I felt this compulsion—the same one I'd felt back then—to work more and more hours and to achieve professional and personal perfection. Somehow I had to make up for all that lost time. I wanted to show the world that I'd beaten this heart thing, at least on the outside. But I wondered if I was doing the right thing. The truth was that I'd never expected my life to be this good again. I never thought I'd have to make any decisions like this, because I didn't think that anyone would be asking me to return to work.

But after six years, I was no longer a burden on my wife, my family, or society in general. I could sleep peacefully at night, knowing that Dakota was there for me. I was still battling my angina, but thanks to Cody's vigilance, I had enough forewarning of the attacks that I didn't have to endure embarrassing blackouts in public places—and I didn't suffer from debilitating depression anymore. I was happy and whole again, and I owed it all to my four-legged angel. But I still owed a lot to my family, too. Was I making the right choices for them, as well as for myself? It's true that Nancy had always been supportive of whatever I wanted to take on, but I owed it to her to really think about these things. Even though I felt ready to take this step, I couldn't do it without Nancy and Dakota taking it with me. And so, with their support, I headed off to Dallas.

The project I was involved in was based out of the Dallas Area Rapid Transit (DART) office in downtown Dallas. DART was a pretty progressive company, and they had no issues with Dakota. In fact, he fit right in, for DART was a public transportation company that worked very hard to accommodate disabled riders and their service dogs.

The people in the DART office knew all about Dakota's alerting abilities. If they hadn't seen it in person, they'd certainly heard about it, either from me or someone else who was there when it happened. There really seemed to be great respect for Cody in the office. Oh sure, they all loved the dog—who doesn't love a golden retriever?—but this was a little more than that.

On a normal day at the office, you could feel a certain amount of tension in the air. Our work was always under some kind of pressure—we tried to meet deadlines, get the best prices, bid a job correctly, deal with cost overruns and change orders, or get suppliers to perform delivery miracles. There were a lot of type-A folks in that office, and we yelled at each other a lot. Most of the time it wasn't personal or vicious; it was just loud. Although it was the reality of our business, it did create an atmosphere that could be difficult at times. My cubicle was the home of one standing joke for the vice presidents and managers. As they headed into a meeting, they'd stop in to see Dakota. "What do you think, Dakota?" they'd ask. "Take a whiff—how do I smell? Can I go into this meeting or should I go home?" They said it jokingly, but most of us knew that there was some reality in what they were saying.

And just about everyone, at one time or another, took comfort in stopping by just to pet Dakota. This was one of the most basic principles of animal-assisted therapy, after all—petting a dog is good for you. It lowers the blood pressure and relaxes your mind and body. I firmly believe that every stressful workplace should have a resident four-legged therapist.

I was happy to share Cody with the office, but he was still working full-time for me—which was a good thing, because those angina attacks kept coming on a fairly regular basis. A lot of them were more bothersome than threatening. The chest pains could be agonizing, but I could fight my way through them. Often, Dakota's role was simply to be there for me to squeeze during the attack and to hold when it was over. He was able to warn me about the major attacks by alerting on me, usually two to five minutes before I could feel them coming. If I was at the office, I had a small room that I could go into to ride out the attacks. The office personnel knew that they were to come and check on me if I wasn't back in a half hour. If I was at home for a major attack, I usually had enough warning from Dakota so I could take my pills, get into bed, and hang on to him until the pain had passed.

The major attacks were excruciating, but Dakota's alerts gave me a head start on getting the medication into my system, which probably prevented the episodes from moving to a major heart attack. And Cody was there for me to squeeze, to transfer my own pain and help regulate my breathing. I believe that he was saving my life every time he alerted on me. Perhaps he was just saving me some pain, but there was no doubt that he'd indeed saved my life on several occasions. And the amazing thing is that, outside of taking a short break once in a while at the office, I missed only a few days of work.

Just when I thought I couldn't be more impressed by Cody's abilities, he surprised me again. An engineer named Bill had a cubicle about fifty feet or so down the hall from mine. We often carpooled to work together, and since Bill and Cody were good buddies, Cody would sometimes wander over to say hello at various times during the day. I think Bill was sneaking him a biscuit now and then, even though he knew that Cody was supposed to be on a diet.

Anyway, I was on my way to a meeting one morning when I called to Dakota. I looked up and saw that he wasn't there. Now, I knew he wouldn't be too far away, as he never ventured beyond where he could I smell or hear me. So I started out, figuring that he must have been making his rounds here in the cubicles, looking for biscuits and pats on the head. I found him with Bill, who was sitting in his chair trying to work. When I got there, Dakota didn't even look up at me—he was pawing away at Bill.

"Cody, I'm not giving you any more cookies. Go with Mike, leave me alone." Bill was chuckling at the situation, but I knew exactly what was going on, and it was no laughing matter.

"Bill, Dakota's alerting on you," I said.

"What?"

"He's alerting on you," I repeated, aware that Bill had a history of heart problems. "Do you feel okay?"

"Mike, I feel fine, but I'll tell you one thing: If Dakota says I'm going to have a heart attack, let's get to the doctor." Bill had seen Dakota in action enough to trust him. He didn't have a heart doctor, so I called my cardiologist, Dr. Gene Henderson.

"Gene, Cody just hit on a guy here at work," I said. "He needs help right now. Can I bring him over?"

Dr. Henderson asked if Bill was in pain.

"Not yet," I told him. "But he does have a history, so I convinced him—Cody convinced him, actually—that he better get to a doctor."

Dr. Henderson knew Cody too, so he said, "Well, get him over here."

We got to Dr. Henderson's office fairly quickly, and Bill still wasn't showing any signs of trouble. He looked at me and said, "Maybe Dakota really did just want a cookie."

For his sake, I hoped that was the case, but I put my faith in Dakota every day. "Well, as long as we're here, let's see what we can find out," I said.

Dr. Henderson's nurse pulled Bill in right away. Cody and I sat in the waiting room, and about fifteen minutes later, I sensed a little commotion in the office. One of the nurses came out to tell me that Bill had suffered a full cardiac arrest on the stress treadmill in the exam room. They had stabilized him, but he was being taken to the hospital.

The next day, Bill had bypass surgery. I was sure that this news, when it got back to the office, would increase the pre-stressful-meeting traffic through my cubicle every morning for checkups from Dakota. Whether or not the people in the office believed that Cody could see their heart difficulties, he certainly was the talk of the office.

But I was still his number-one customer. One June night in 1999, Dakota jumped into bed with me at five A.M. and exhibited alerting behavior, even though I was fast asleep. He persisted in this, which drew Nancy's attention. She tried to wake me, but didn't get a response, so she called 911 right away. As it turns out, I was having a full-blown heart attack in my sleep. My blood pressure had dropped to sixty over thirty-eight, and without Cody's alert, I would never have awakened that morning. My recollection of the event was understandably somewhat hazy, but Nancy told me that Cody stayed right there to comfort me, never moving from the bed.

I do have one very real, clear, and vivid memory of that morning. I couldn't move, but at one point I opened my eyes and saw Dakota looking right at me. In his blue-gray eyes were two gold angels. For all the comfort that he'd given me, for all the special time that we'd spent together, for all the conversations that we'd shared, this was the first time that I had seen anything like this. What did it mean? I took it as a sign that I was surrounded by a very special presence, that I was being watched over by some greater power, and that everything was going to be all right. I remember feeling warm all over, and I was reassured that I would survive this crisis.

And I did survive. I took a little time off from work, but I was soon back in the office. Dakota was once again a calming presence for everyone. He was a very real, lifesaving hero for many. . . but especially for me.

Chosen by

a Dog

Caleb

Marion Bond West

Absolutely no! Not now, not next year, never," I told Jeremy, one of our thirteen-year-old twins. Since we'd been forced to have our magnificent collie put to sleep after she was hit by a car and badly injured nine months ago, I had refused even to discuss another dog. With God's help I had got through the pain of Mollie's death, but I was determined never to suffer that way again.

No more dogs for me. I no longer watched the side of the road for strays to rescue, or petted dogs that wandered through our yard. Even though the rest of the family—my husband Jerry, our boys Jon and Jeremy, and our nineteen-year-old daughter Jennifer—desperately wanted another dog, I held out stubbornly. They might be able to love again, but I was not.

Sometimes, though, I found my eyes wandering to the want ads, just "checking" to see if there were collies for sale. For a few seconds I would allow myself to think about having a dog again—but I would quickly push the idea aside. I would have nothing to do with dogs—ever.

But as hard as I fought it, something was stirring inside me. Almost daily I envisioned a beautiful collie out back—

running, jumping, sleeping, even looking in the window at me, its tail wagging. For almost nine months this went on—and it became a joyful habit. When it snowed unexpectedly one day, in my mind a collie pranced in our white backyard. Often when I'd drive into the carport, I'd envision the collie there greeting me. After supper, when there were scraps left over, I mentally gave them to a dog with a long nose and soft brown eyes.

One warm, sunny winter day, my husband went out to the spot where he liked to stretch out on the dry, soft grass. Jerry looked so alone out there without Mollie—she had always followed and sprawled on top of him. In an instant, in my mind, I saw a collie appear—and pounce.

I suppose I missed Mollie most of all early in the morning. That had been our special time together. I'd open the back door just after the sun was up, and she'd be there in a flash, tail wagging. I would sit on the step and she'd put her head in my lap. I'd stroke her long nose and say, "I love you, Mollie Sunshine." Every morning in my mind she was there, waiting to start our day together.

By now I wasn't certain if I was remembering Mollie or imagining a new dog. It didn't seem to matter. The images were comforting, and I could handle a collie who just lived in my mind.

Early one morning, just before time for the school bus, I heard Jon and Jeremy shouting excitedly in front of the house. Holding my robe tightly around me, I hurried out the door and down the steps onto our front lawn. I stopped. There, to my astonishment, stood the collie of my imagination. It could have been Mollie or Mollie's twin—just standing there wagging its tail!

We all seemed to freeze. The boys didn't move or speak. The dog stood perfectly still too—even its tail was motionless. I think I might have stopped breathing for a few seconds.

The dog didn't have a collar. The fur underneath its stomach was crusted with mud. He was much too thin and appeared exhausted. But this dog wasn't just an image in my mind; he was real!

I dropped to my knees, flung my arms around the collie and buried my face in its thick fur. Suddenly, something gave way inside of me, and in that instant I knew that the love I'd felt for Mollie wasn't meant to be locked up inside, but meant to flow outward and onward, no matter what happened.

The dog licked my face over and over and put out a paw for shaking. My mind was asking, *Where did you come from? How did you get here?* But my heart was pounding, *Welcome, welcome!*

"Will you feed him, Mama?" Jon asked.

"Of course," I said. "There's the bus, you'd better hurry."

The dog followed me into the backyard almost as though things were familiar to him. He ran around and around in a circle right in Mollie's old tracks. He checked out the doghouse and drank from Mollie's water pan, which we still kept full for the cat.

Can this be? I thought. This dog was doing everything that the dog of my imagination had done. I even had the funny feeling that maybe he'd been somewhere imagining a big yard to play in and a family to adore him.

I fed the hungry visitor almost everything in the house. Finally he lay down under the oak tree and slept. Back in the kitchen, I stood and watched him. He was there, he was really there.

When our cat Joshua ventured out back, the two appeared to be old friends. *Joshua and Caleb*, I thought to myself, remembering what good friends the biblical Joshua and Caleb had been. From then on I called the stray collie "Caleb."

Of course, I knew we had to try to find the owner. But I had this delicious premonition that there wasn't one to find. I called all the vets in the area and waited to see if they had any record of a missing collie. Each time the answer came back over the phone, I breathed a sigh of relief and a prayer of gratitude. I checked with the Humane Society and the pound, leaving my name and number at each location. Then I ran an ad in the paper for a week. The days passed and no one called to claim our Caleb.

I have no reasonable explanation as to where the collie came from or how he got to our house. But somehow I'll always believe that "seeing" a collie daily in our yard for so long when none was there had something powerful to do with Caleb's finding us.

Caleb's arrival has taught me that often the very thing you try to avoid is the exact thing you need the most. Even though I didn't consciously pray for another collie, I believe God knew the desire of my heart and what I really needed even before I asked. And if someday Caleb is taken from us, I know that God will once again be there to help me through the pain and grief, and prepare the way for new happiness.

Now Caleb and I start each day together. Early in the morning I slip out the back door and Caleb is waiting, just as Mollie used to be. I sit on the steps and he moves as close as he can and puts his head in my lap. We sit there in the sun together, and I rub his long, soft nose and say, "I love you, Caleb."

What a relief it is to let love flow freely again, and to know with a certainty that—just as it says in Psalm 30:5—weeping often endures for a night, but joy comes in the morning!

The Dog in
the Woods

Diane Wills

I was brand-new to the real estate business the first time I visited the long-abandoned rural house I was trying to sell for an out-of-state mortgage company. The property was in Brunswick County, North Carolina, practically in the middle of nowhere. I was putting up a For Sale sign, the hammer echoes blending with the whine of the cicadas, when the feeling struck me: someone, or something, was watching.

My hammer paused in mid swing. I thought I saw a movement in the scraggly undergrowth behind the house. There it was again. That time I was sure. In the woods was a dog. Even from a distance I could see he was mangy and undernourished. He panted heavily in the thick humidity. Nothing's stickier than a mid-August day in coastal Carolina. *I wonder if the house still has running water,* I thought, but one step and the dog melted into the woods without a sound.

While driving back to the office, winding along the dusty country roads, I wondered about the animal. Two weeks before, Hurricane Bertha had walloped Wilmington, tearing a broad swath of devastation. Was that dog a refugee from the nightmare storm? Had he ridden out the gale in those woods?

A few days later I went back to the house to meet with a mowing service to arrange to have the brush cleared and grass cut. Once again I had the eerie sensation of being watched. When I glanced into the woods, there he was, in almost the same spot. I called, "C'mon, boy!" But he vanished at the sound of my voice.

"People-shy," the lawn man commented. "You'll never get near him."

I had half a ham sandwich left over from lunch. Pulling it out of my bag, I tossed it into the brush, and the dog emerged and pounced on it ravenously. I was able to get a closer look at him. His fur had fallen out in clumps, except for on his head and legs, where it was dull and matted. His back was covered with sores. His eyes shifted furtively. He gobbled my offering, then was gone.

That night at dinner I mentioned him to my husband, John. "It's best you stay away from him," John advised. "Probably wild."

"But he must have belonged to someone once," I protested. I just couldn't understand how anyone could abandon a dog.

"Don't get any ideas," John warned. "We've got a full house." He was referring to our schnauzer, Max, and Minnie, a calico cat. All I could muster in response was a noncommittal sigh.

That week at my Wednesday prayer meeting I hesitated to talk about the dog in the woods. After all, people were concerned with serious life issues—health problems, divorce, finances, job loss. What business did I have asking prayers for an animal? Yet I couldn't get him off my mind. Finally, at the end of the meeting, I said, "I'm sorry if this sounds trivial, but I would like to ask prayers for a stray dog who's living behind a house I'm trying to sell."

To my relief, everyone smiled and nodded. Our minister, Jeff Douglas, rested his hand on my shoulder. "Remember, he's one of God's creatures too," he said.

The dog was put on our regular prayer list. As word got around, he was added to friends' and neighbors' lists as well, and people asked me about him from time to time. A couple of days a week I found an excuse to visit the property, and brought along a bag of kibble and a bowl. I set the food at the edge of the brush and from a distance watched the dog eat. He always seemed tense and hyperalert, eyeing me warily as he devoured the kibble, backing off if I got close, his fear even more powerful than his hunger. I wished he would trust me not to harm him. Yet I dared not venture too close, afraid of scaring him off, maybe for good.

One day John caught me red-handed, loading the trunk of my car with kibble and treats. "Diane . . . " he said sternly. I slammed the lid. "You know we can't take on another pet," he went on. "With my retirement and your just getting started in real estate, we have enough to worry about."

"I know. I just don't want him to starve," I said as I drove off.

The truth was, I didn't know what I wanted. Mainly, I wanted the stray to be all right. I wanted to stop worrying about him. I didn't want him to be so scared of people that no one could help him. I knew we couldn't take in another animal, but I couldn't stand by and do nothing while the poor creature wasted away. *Dear Lord,* I begged, *I feel so bad for that dog. Please help me find a solution.*

Meanwhile, I wasn't having much luck selling the house. At least that allowed me to keep visiting the dog. Weeks passed. I tried to drop by as often as was practicable. Sometimes I saw him and sometimes I didn't. Usually he was skittish and hungry, as if he didn't know how to find food on his own. Then, six weeks after I first spotted the dog in the woods, the National Weather Service issued an alert: a hurricane was bearing down on the North Carolina coast, maybe even bigger than Bertha. *He's all alone out there,* I thought.

We began to prepare for the worst—boarding up windows, stockpiling emergency supplies. One thing I had to do was go around and pull up all my For Sale signs. In gale winds they can become deadly projectiles. As I drove out to Brunswick County, racing ahead of a plum, marbled sky, I was tormented by worry. *He's survived one hurricane. Can he possibly survive another?* How could I convince him to come with me to safety? *Lord, he has to trust me!*

When I got to the house, the rain was coming down in

wind-whipped sheets. I didn't see the dog anywhere. After I pulled up the sign I took a bowl of kibble to the edge of the brush. Saying a prayer, I put it on the ground and piled heavy rocks around it. I stood up, the wind buffeting me. One last look.

And there he was, just five feet away, closer than ever before. I stood stock-still even as a clap of thunder crashed overhead. Our eyes met. Then I turned and calmly walked back to my car, opened the trunk, took out a blanket I kept there and spread it out on the back seat. I stole a glance over my shoulder. He was still there. Staring.

I faced the dog. "If you want some help," I said, pointing to the open car door, "please get in."

The trees seemed to bend as one, choreographed by the wind. Then the dog was moving toward me, past me, and nimbly into the back seat.

"Good boy!"

Back home, my husband's resolve broke down as soon as he set eyes on the bedraggled refugee. We put the dog in the bathtub. He was covered with sores and nasty ticks, but he didn't struggle or bite when we washed him, though I knew the soap must have stung something awful. He bore it all stoically. "Good boy," I kept chanting soothingly as I dried him. The storm was poised just off the coast. I took advantage of the respite and rushed the dog over to our vet, Dr. Deborah Wicks.

"Diane," she said, "this dog has the worst case of mange and insect bites I have ever seen. Good thing you got him."

Treatment would be costly, and I doubted John and I could afford it. Right then, I just wanted to get the dog help. "Do what you can," I told the vet as I left. We would decide what the next step was after the hurricane passed. *It's up to you, God. . . .*

Rain swept across our driveway as I drove up. John was bringing in camping lanterns and the phone was ringing. I rushed past him to get it.

"Hello?"

It was Dr. Wicks's assistant, Shannon Hewitt. Yes, the dog was doing fine. Shannon was cleaning his sores and giving him a special medicated bath. She thought he was going to pull through okay. "Listen," she said, hesitating. "I don't know if you and Mr. Wills are planning to keep him, but the truth is I've been praying for a dog to come along. Not just any dog, but one who really needs a home and the kind of love my little boy and I could give. This guy here is pretty special. It would be an answer to prayer if I could keep him."

I had to stop myself from crying. Because Shannon worked at the vet's, the cost of treatment would be substantially reduced. John and I could help her out. Together we could swing it.

"What are you going to name him?" I finally composed myself enough to ask.

"After what he's been through, I think I'll call him Gamut."

Gamut made it through Hurricane Fran just fine. Today he has a lustrous coat, as black as coal. He's healthy

117

and he loves people. He couldn't have a better home. When I stop over to visit, he offers me a paw and throws his head back. I know he's grateful because I feel the same way. Grateful for the prayers of neighbors and friends, and for a God who looks after all his creatures.

The Stray

Lynelle Whitney

The last thing I was looking for that Fourth of July Saturday was a dog. All I wanted was to get through the day. My husband, Mike, and I had just finished lunch. I'd managed to bring the dishes into the kitchen. I'd do them later—maybe. I pushed open the screen door and stepped out into our front yard, letting the summer day envelop me. The day was gorgeous, the sky a deep clear blue. For a moment, the blanket of fear and anxiety I lived under lifted. *Lord, why can't I learn to enjoy my life more? Why can't I just get better?*

Mike and I had moved here to rural Pennsylvania from just outside New York City. Our jobs in New York were burning us out. "Mike," I'd said one day, "let's make a new start in Pennsylvania. Relax a little."

Mike got a carpentry job in nearby Harrisburg. For the first time since I was a teenager, I had all the time I wanted to putter around at home, savoring life in the country.

Except I couldn't relax. I didn't know what to do with all the free time. My mind filled up with images of things that could go wrong—terrifying scenarios that I knew were totally irrational, yet I couldn't shake off. *Stop it,* I'd tell myself a dozen times a day. *You're not being reasonable.* The more I struggled, the worse it got.

I'd lie in bed at night, one worry after another wrapping itself around me, almost squeezing the life out of me. Days, weeks, then months blurred together. In the morning I'd force myself to get out of bed. Most days I got no farther than the sofa in our living room. And that's where Mike would find me when he got home from work. No dinner waiting for him, no cleaning or gardening done. *Mike deserves much better. He is knocking himself out every day and I'm doing nothing. I've got to snap out of this.* I prayed, but the more I felt like I was letting Mike down, the more the anxieties themselves felt like a punishment for not getting better.

Everything around me became a potential danger; each new situation, a disaster just waiting to happen. By that Fourth of July Saturday, I'd been living in my fear for so long that it was hard to remember when things had ever been different. I wanted to get better. I really did. I just didn't know how.

I stood out front, looking up the road. What was that by the edge of the woods? A dog—medium-sized, with short, coppery fur—emerged from the trees. I knew all the dogs in the area, and I'd never seen this one before. *It must be a stray.* The fur on the dog's chest was discolored. *Mange?* The dog turned in to our drive. He was heading right for me.

I backed into the house and called down to the basement. "Mike! There's a strange dog out here. I think he needs help." Translation: *You need to get up here and do something. Now.*

I went out front again. The dog was limping away, down the road. In a moment he would be out of sight. *He needs help.* "Here, boy!" I heard myself call out.

He stopped, turned around and came back toward the house—toward me.

That wasn't mange on the dog's fur. It was blood—lots of it. It covered his chest and ran freely down his legs. I slipped back inside and shut the screen door.

This is too much. I can't deal with this. On a good day, just getting the mail or doing the laundry was a challenge. Whatever was wrong with that dog, it was way more than I could handle. *I'm sorry, Lord. I want to help him.*

The dog walked up and sat down in front of the door, its tail tentatively thumping against the ground.

"Mike!" I yelled. "Come up here!"

The dog and I stared at each other through the screen. Blood poured from his mouth and nose. He labored for breath. Yet he seemed calm, tranquil almost.

My gaze locked on those liquid brown eyes. The trust in them was so complete, so unquestioning, that I couldn't turn away. "Don't worry," I said through the screen. "You're going to be all right. We're going to take care of you."

Mike came up behind me. The second he saw the shape the dog was in, he snapped into action. Grabbing a blanket from the closet, he brushed past me and draped it over the poor creature. He was doing something, as usual—while I stood by.

Suddenly I saw the whole situation. I'd been standing by

that door the way I'd been going through life—as if my feet were nailed to the floor. It was time to take action, time to stop being a prisoner of my fears. That dog had the courage to trust that we were going to help him. Now I just had to believe that God would help me. I had to stop doubting God and start trusting him. *All right, Lord, I know you're going to help me help this dog. That's why he's here.*

I ran into the living room, got out the phone book, and dialed the nearest vet. A machine came on. "We've got a badly injured stray dog here," I said. "He's covered in blood." I left my number. A few minutes later, the vet called back.

"I understand you want to help," he said. "But I can't treat a dog if I don't know who the owner is. I've gotten into trouble for that."

"Doctor," I said, "this is a real emergency. The dog is bleeding to death right here in my front yard."

"Okay, okay. I'll meet you at my office."

I ran back out just as Mike was loading the dog into the back of our truck. Ten minutes later, we pulled up to the veterinarian's office. He was standing out front, waiting for us.

"It's a gunshot wound," the vet told us twenty minutes later, holding up an x-ray. "He's lost a lot of blood. But he could still pull through."

Amazingly, the dog had never struggled, never resisted. Wounded and bloody, with his life ebbing away, he'd just kept looking at us—at me—with those trusting, accepting eyes.

First thing the next morning, I called the vet. It was Sunday, but I prayed someone might pick up. An assistant answered. "He's doing great," she told me. "He's been for a walk already this morning, and he had something to eat."

Early Monday morning, I went to the vet's office. The moment Rusty, as I'd christened the dog, saw me, he ran directly to me. He jumped up, put his paws at my waist and buried his head against my stomach in a long, quiet hug. With his wounds stitched up and the blood cleaned away, he looked like a different animal. Except for those eyes. They had the same unmistakable look in them. *I knew you could do it*, they almost seemed to say.

"He's a wonderful dog," the vet said. "He should be easy to find a home for."

"Find a home?" I said, reaching out and giving Rusty a scratch behind his ear. "That won't be necessary. He's coming with us. I have things to learn from him."

It had started with a simple lesson two days before: When you doubt God, you'll doubt yourself. Trust God, and you'll believe in yourself.

Little Dog Found

Aletha Jane Lindstrom

I saw her first in mid-December during one of Michigan's cruelest winters. She was running across the frozen barnyard, a small ghost of a dog, almost obliterated from sight by swirling snow.

Living in the country, we've become accustomed to seeing abandoned dogs and cats. We seldom see the same one twice, but this one was strangely different. My husband, Andy, and I glimpsed her frequently—in the barnyard, the fields, the woods, along the road. And she was always running, head held high, either trying desperately to find someone or fleeing in abject terror.

My heart went out to the small creature. How could she possibly survive the bitter cold? Even Collie, our big farm dog, who loves winter, was content to remain indoors.

But the plight of the little lost dog provided only brief distraction from the black mood that engulfed me. My dad had died recently and it had been hard to let him go. Though I was sustained by God's promise that we'll be reunited with our loved ones, lately there had been dark times when my faith flickered. Could I trust God's promise? The question gnawed at me. For a while I prayed about it, then stopped.

On one below-zero evening, as I walked down the drive for the newspaper, I sensed I was being followed. I looked back, and there was the lost dog—a small beagle with big freckled feet, a wagging tail, and soft, pleading eyes. I removed my mitten, but before I could touch her, she cowered and drew back. Then she panicked and fled into the woods, leaving bloody footprints in the snow.

I couldn't sleep that night; the memory of those eyes haunted me. Had she been stolen for hunting and later abandoned? Where was she now? Had she found shelter from the bitter cold, or was she still running, terrified and alone?

The next morning we followed tracks in the woods until we found her. Andy held out a piece of meat and she crept toward it on her belly. When she drew close enough, I grabbed her. She struggled and cried until her strength was gone. Then she lay whimpering in my arms.

We wrapped her in a blanket and took her to the vet. "Poor little mutt," I said as we carried her in. "He'll probably have to put her down."

The vet removed the blanket, now bloodstained, and ran gentle, capable hands over the dog's emaciated body. The head, it seemed, was permanently tipped to one side. She was covered with cuts, welts, and scars, and the pads were worn from her feet. "She's either been running for days over frozen ground or digging to make a bed in the leaves—probably both," he said.

Silently we awaited the verdict. "She's a good little beagle," he said at last. "I think we can save her."

"Then I'd better advertise for the owner," I said.

"I wouldn't bother," the vet replied. "She's smart. If she's from around here, she'd have found her way home—that is, if she'd wanted to go. . . ."

"But she's so frightened. How long before she'll get over that?"

"Never—not entirely. Apparently she's been badly abused. When that happens, a dog becomes either vicious or afraid for the rest of its life." His voice softened. "And obviously this little dog will never be vicious."

"You mean she'll even be afraid of us?"

"Probably." He was silent for a moment and then added thoughtfully, "But we can't be sure. Sometimes love works wonders."

That night I brought a dog bed from the attic and placed it near the kitchen stove. To my surprise she crept in immediately, settled down with a long sigh, and closed her eyes. For the first time the trembling stopped.

I knelt beside her, my mind filled with questions. This small stranger, seemingly from nowhere—why had she approached me in the drive, pleading for affection? And why, needing it so much, had she fled in terror when I offered it? It seemed we had something in common: We were both afraid to trust.

Gently I stroked the soft ears. "You can trust us, Puppy," I whispered. "You needn't be afraid—ever again." I placed an old shawl over her and tucked it around her, making sure it would stay.

"It seems we have ourselves another dog," Andy said the next morning.

I nodded. "I'm not sure I'm happy about it. Now that Tim's away from home, I figured we wouldn't get another dog . . . after Collie. They all die and break your heart sooner or later." *That's the way with love*, I thought, remembering Dad.

"Let's forget the heartaches," Andy said gently, "and remember the happy times. They've given us so many of them."

He was right, of course. I couldn't imagine life without a dog. Besides, I'd already succumbed to this one. She was so hurt and frightened, so little and alone. And she needed us so desperately. Her eyes, her most endearing feature, were dark puddles, reflecting her emotions. I longed to see them shining with eagerness and love—as a little dog's eyes should be.

We continued calling her "Puppy." Somehow it seemed to fit. I remembered what the vet said about her fear, but I couldn't believe she'd be afraid of us. She was, though. She allowed us to minister to her injuries, but when we reached out to pet her, she cringed and pulled away, as if she feared we would strike her. I wondered if perhaps that was why her head was tipped.

We gave up trying to pet her. "She'll come to us when she's ready to trust us," I said. But the rejection hurt. I wondered if that's the way God feels about us when we fail to trust him.

Andy, unaware of my thoughts, said, "She'll learn. It's a beagle's nature to be happy and affectionate."

"Love casteth out fear," I said, quoting 1 John 4:18. Here was another of God's promises. Could I believe this one?

Weeks passed and Puppy didn't respond. Collie seemed to be her only security. I usually walked Collie down the lane in late afternoon. When Puppy's paws were healed, she joined us. Sometimes she'd wander off, following a scent. But when she discovered she was alone, she'd race back to Collie.

Those were the good days. There were other, heartbreaking ones when the beagle seemed to be in a trance. She'd wander to the roadside and huddle there, a solitary figure, gazing up and down. I'd send Collie to bring her back. Inside she took to her bed, her eyes confused and unseeing. I'd sit by her and slip my hand under her chin. "Is there someone you love, Puppy? Someone you've been searching for?"

At such times I wished I knew where she'd come from, what she'd experienced. Then, looking at the sad eyes and the ugly scars, I decided I'd rather not know.

By late spring I noticed changes in her behavior. Her trips to the roadside grew fewer, and she waited as impatiently as Collie did for our walks. There were times too, when we were petting Collie, that she'd draw close and watch wistfully. And that was the way things remained.

Then one September afternoon I leaned on the back fence, watching our two dogs. They were in the far side of a back field engaged in a recently discovered pastime, chasing grasshoppers. Collie hunted with her eyes, leaping on her prey. Puppy hunted with her nose, snuffling along the ground. Only her waving white-tipped tail was visible above the weeds.

I watched in amusement. The little dog had been with us eight months now, but she was still afraid and still wouldn't come to be petted. Despite our hopes and our prayers, love hadn't worked its magic after all. Yet just having the small dog and knowing she was enjoying life lent pleasure to my days.

Collie saw me and came running. I knelt and put my arms around her, my eyes still on the waving white-tipped tail moving in the maze of weeds. Suddenly Puppy discovered she was alone. She darted in frantic circles until she caught Collie's scent. Then she came racing toward us.

When she reached us, she pushed her eager, squirming body between Collie and me. She looked up, her eyes shining with that soft light that comes only from the heart. *Me too!* they plainly said. *Love me too!*

"I do love you, Puppy. I'll always love you," I said, snuggling her close. So love had cast out fear, just as the promise says. "It's all right, Dad," I whispered. A gladness was rising in me that I hadn't felt for a long time. I knew then that God is faithful to all his promises.

Fantasy Dog

Caroline Knapp

The puppy—Lucille at ten weeks—is stalking an ant. She creeps along the edge of the fence on my patio, head tucked low, neck stretched forward, her step delicate and calculated and silent. I can't see the ant so I'm not exactly sure what she's doing, but I can see the intensity of her focus. She stops, her gaze fixed at something about two feet ahead; her body tenses, and then she pounces: lunges forward, lands, and stops, front paws planted on the brick, hindquarters raised, little curl of a tail swishing behind her.

I watch this, and I smile. (And smile and smile and smile.) In the course of two weeks, this creature has crawled into a corner of my heart and gotten lodged there—permanent occupancy. I look at her, and sometimes I have to clench my teeth to keep from grabbing her and squishing her, she so delights me. *Where did you come from?* I gaze at her, wondering this. *How did I end up with you?*

Good questions; I'm still asking them today. I stumbled into the world of dogs with major blinders on, just kind of woke up one day with this animal in my house. This is not an exaggeration, either—I've acquired toasters with more deliberation than I acquired Lucille. One fantasy, one ani-

mal shelter, fifty bucks, puppy. In retrospect, I'm also astonished by this: I'm not by nature a spontaneous person, and
I'm certainly not a rash one, so the idea that I'd just go out
one afternoon and come home with a live animal seems
completely out of character. But fate has an uncanny way of
giving you what you need, presenting you with the right les-
sons at the precise moment you're ready to learn them. At
the time I needed to learn a lot—about connection and
closeness and safety—and something deep inside whispered,
A dog, you need a dog, and I was lucky enough, or open
enough, to listen.

A few weeks before I got Lucille, I'd been sitting at a
table outside a café in Cambridge with my friend Susan,
watching a trio of people and a dog at a nearby table. The
dog, a medium-size mixed-breed with intelligent eyes, was
sweet-looking in a mangy way; and he sat next to his owner
with that patient, contented look that some dogs seem to
wear all the time: ears relaxed, eyes bright, mouth partway
open in a mild pant that looked like a smile. At one point
the dog stood up and started to wander away from the table.
The owner whistled lightly, and the dog stopped, looked
over his shoulder, then trotted back to the table and rested
his head on the owner's knee. The owner gave him a soft
pat, then returned to his coffee. The two looked utterly at
home together, man and dog.

I watched this with vague envy, the way I might watch a
couple holding hands. "I want a dog," I said to Susan, nodding
in the pair's direction. "I'm thinking about getting a dog."

This was the first time I'd said the words aloud, although in the days and weeks before I got Lucille, I'd been aware that dog thoughts had been circling in the back of my mind: dog fantasies, a kind of low-grade puppy lust.

Ask ten people why they want a dog, or why they got one, and you will get ten variations on the same theme: Dog equals love. More to the point, dog equals a very specific brand of love: a warm-and-fuzzy variety, pure and simple, low-maintenance and relatively risk free. A dog will return us to more idyllic times, to summer afternoons we spent romping with the family dog as children. A dog will do for us what Lassie did for Timmy—provide constancy and protection and solace, our very own saint in the backyard. A dog will curl at our feet and gaze up at us adoringly, will fetch our paper in the morning and our slippers come nightfall, will serve us and love us without question or demand. This is Walt Disney love, rose-colored and light and tender, and the wish for it lurks within every human soul, the dog owner's being no exception.

People tend to be surprisingly vague when they talk about why they decided to get a dog—I've been struck by this countless times. You'll ask, "Why a dog?" and "Why then? Why did you get a dog at that particular time in your life?" and you'll often get a highly generic response, or a pragmatic one. A mother of two boys echoes the parental refrain when she tells me, "We got the dog for the kids." A retired schoolteacher in Washington cites the fitness-and-activity rationale: "I wanted a pet that would get me out-doors, give me a reason to get out of the house for walks." In interviews dozens of dog owners in varying categories—single women, single men, married couples—trotted out variations of an even less-specific theme: "I don't know, I just like dogs. I grew up with dogs and I always wanted one."

Those are all valid, perfectly reasonable responses—dogs can be great playmates for children; dogs will get you out of the house for walks; dogs are, or at least can be, eminently likable—but I think people tend to be vague because getting a dog can be such an intensely personal matter, all tied up with that Disney ideal, and the very personal fantasies and yearnings that lurk behind it. Even the most pragmatic rationales contain deeper hopes. The family dog offers the promise of stability: the house in the suburbs, the picket fence, the golden retriever in the back of the station wagon. The outdoor dog offers the promise of fidelity and companionship: the trusted Lab trotting by your side. The statement "I grew up with dogs" suggests a longing for the purity and innocence of childhood bonds, a wish for simpler times and less cluttered relationships. Dogs strike deep chords in us, ones that are bolstered by the individual experiences of childhood, by the culture at large, and by history. Humans have lived with dogs for thousands of years, after all, and our ideals about them are deeply rooted, bred into the dog-loving portion of the population as surely as the instinct to chase prey has been bred into hounds. We've rhapsodized about dogs in literature and poetry, filled centuries worth of canvases with images of their nobility and strength, celebrated their loyalty and steadfastness in film; from Odysseus's Argus, who waited longer than Penelope, to the long-distance loyalty of Lassie, we have exalted the dog for attributes all-too-often absent from human affairs.

Of course, I didn't set out to fill those longings deliberately. Certainly I didn't sit back one day and think: *Gee, I've lost both parents and quit drinking and my life is full of gaping holes; guess it's time to get a puppy.* Instead, I woke up on a Sunday morning in August, an unplanned day looming before me, and I thought: *What the heck. Maybe I'll go to the pound and just look.* I wasn't sufficiently wedded to the idea of a dog to launch a full-scale investigation of breeds and breeders, and I had an instinctive aversion to pet-store puppies (a good instinct, as it turns out, since an alarming proportion of pet-store dogs come from puppy mills, which churn them out for volume and profit and with little regard for health or breeding). I also liked the idea of rescuing a dog, so I mulled the notion over, and I got up off my sofa and headed out the door.

One thing I've noticed since I quit drinking is that a person usually has two or three sets of impulses scratching away at some internal door at any given time. If you're sober—if you're alert, and paying attention to those impulses, and not yielding to the instinct to anesthetize them—you can receive a lot of guidance about where to go, what to do next in life. Some people in AA define this as their higher power, as though there's a part of each of us, a kind of higher self, that wants to be healthy and well, that can set us on the right path if only we heed its messages. I felt that scratching that morning, as though an invisible thread were attached to my soul and tugging at me ever so gently. *Do it. Just go look.* Of course, the part of me that wants to resist a healthy impulse can be incredibly strong; so, looking back, I'm still surprised that I actually got in my car and came home with a puppy. But the thread kept tugging, and I managed not to dismiss it.

I drove out to Sudbury, Massachusetts, where my sister lived, and she took me to an animal shelter near her house. We didn't find anything there—the kennel consisted of about two dozen pens, a dozen on each side of a long hall, and none of the dogs struck me in quite the right way. There were some large, loud, lunging dogs who looked like too much to take on; a few small, hyper-looking dogs who seemed too high-strung and yippy; and a few others who were too old, or too funny looking, or too sickly, or somehow just not what I had in mind. It's a weird feeling, walking down a hallway of rejected animals and rejecting them all over again, and the experience made me feel guilty and uncomfortable, as though I lacked some requisite degree of altruism or humanity. That feeling gnawed at me and almost turned me off the idea entirely, but when I got back to my sister's house, the thread tugged again. *Go somewhere else.* And so it was that, an hour later, I walked into the Animal Rescue League in downtown Boston, equipped with the ID and documentation required to adopt a pet, ready, I guess, to find my dog.

Lucille is a remarkably serene dog, poised even as a puppy, and that struck me about her from the start. When I first saw her, she was in a small cage in a corner of the shelter, with barking, yelping, yowling dogs on all sides. A spaniel in the cage beside hers kept charging at its cage door, up and back, up and back. A large husky mix in a bigger cage barked and clawed at the door. Eyes beseeched; nails scratched against metal; I found myself not wanting to look. But there she was. Amid all the noise and chaos, Lucille was lying calmly in her cage with a pink chew toy between her front paws. She looked utterly focused on that chew toy, as though she was quite capable of entertaining herself, thank you, and didn't need to claw and clamor for attention like the others; and the sight of that appealed to me in a visceral way: it spoke to a kind of grace under pressure, a quality of endurance that I suppose I was looking to cultivate in my own life.

Still, she was not my ideal of the perfect dog, at least not in an obvious way. My aesthetic ideal tends toward the sleek and muscular: Rhodesian ridgebacks and Doberman pinschers. I like big dogs, athletic dogs; and in the days and weeks before I got Lucille, I'd formed a picture of an elegant animal with wide, searching eyes and a fine coat, short-haired and suede-like and earth-toned, a dog (here's an embarrassingly telling concern) that would match my furniture. Lucille does not look like this, nor did she promise to as a puppy. An information-bearing card over her cage identified her simply as a "shepherd mix," which I've come to understand is a euphemism for "We really have no idea." Looking at her that first day, I couldn't tell if she'd grow up to be beautiful or homely. She had dainty paws and nice proportions for a pup; but she was a bit on the runty side, her coat was a somewhat mousy brown, and she looked like she might be kind of stumpy when she grew up, her legs too short for her body. Mostly she was tiny and funny looking, like an oversized rodent. I stood there looking at her. *My dog? I am not at all sure.*

I crouched down at the cage and watched her. She looked up happily enough, and I poked my finger between the bars. She gave it a curious sniff. Lucille has shepherd ears, and they were flopped over at the time, two small triangles pointing in either direction. Very cute, but I still didn't fall in love with her right then and there. I sat and thought: *Can I do this?*

This was one of those crossroads moments, when you understand that something potentially life-altering is in front of you, and you know you could go either way—take the plunge and upset everything or cast a vote for stasis and go home to your sofa. A woman I know named Helen first saw her dog, a now-four-year-old Cairn terrier whom she adores, in the window of a pet store, when passing by on her way to meet a friend for lunch. She stood at the window and looked at him. She went in, looked more closely, poked her finger through the bars of the cage the same way I did. The puppy licked her hand, wagged his tail. She left, went back, left again. Then she spent the entire lunch obsessed with the idea, dragged her friend in and out of the pet store, and walked around the block four times. She still doesn't know what tipped the scales for her, but she remembers the questions: *Should I? Shouldn't I? Can I? Why? Why not?*

The scales in my case went up and down (and up and down again) on the matter of puppyhood, the responsibility it implied. After a lot of circling, my dog thoughts had landed on the side of caution, and I pretty much figured I'd get a mature dog, maybe a year or two old, who'd arrive housetrained and equipped with a mastery of the basic commands. Naive as that logic seems to me today, it sounded like an easy enough adjustment at the time: just let the dog in, learn its ways, incorporate it into my routines. But something about seeing a puppy, so small and undeveloped, also spoke to those yearnings of mine, to the part of me that seemed to want a deeper sort of experience, a fuller involvement, a relationship that might feel more special somehow.

Special. That's what I really wondered about: *Can I do special? Can I love this creature the way she's meant to be loved? Can I get her to love me? Am I capable of forming the right sort of relationship here, creating the kind of bond I saw between the man and dog at the café that day? I tend to be such a fearful person when it comes to intimacy, so self-protective and locked into my routines, so averse to commitment. How would a small vulnerable pup affect all that?*

A few minutes passed. A shelter employee came up to

me while I was kneeling at Lucille's cage and told me I could take her out and play with her a bit if I filled out an adoption form first. I went into an adjoining reception area and did that; she came out a few minutes later carrying Lucille in her arms. Lucille's head rested on the woman's shoulders, and she was looking around the room in a curious, peaceful way, a picture of trust and composure. The employee handed her to me, and we settled down in a corner, me sitting cross-legged on the floor and Lucille sliding about in front of me on the linoleum. She looked calm and active and alert, happy to be out of the cage and able to sniff about freely. She sniffed here and she sniffed there, puppy nails scratching on the floor. I watched her. I debated. *Can I do this? I'm not sure I can do this. Can I?*

Just then, Lucille did a little canine jig, lifting her two front paws one after the other and sort of hurling her whole body forward on the floor into a play bow—one of those tiny motions that's so cute, it looks like a parody of puppy behavior. Then she squatted down and peed on the floor, a yellow puddle widening beneath her. My dog trainer once asked me why I chose Lucille—why her, out of all the other potential puppies in the universe—and that image sprang to mind: a little puppy making a big old mess. The sight struck some note of familiarity in me. No one at the shelter knew where Lucille had come from or why she'd been abandoned. She'd been left there the day before—no litter mates, no explanation, no story. And looking back, I can see that she looked exactly like I felt: unmoored, in need of care, a young female pup unattached to home or family. I suppose that's what clinched the decision for me. Her vulnerability spoke to my deepest fantasy: together we would form an attachment, create some semblance of home and family, a pack of two.

I stood up, walked over to the shelter employee, and said, "I'll take her."

One Red Hound

Kat Albrecht
with Jana Murphy

When I entered the police academy, I knew I would get a bloodhound as soon as I graduated. In fact, the opportunity to be paid to work with search dogs was my whole reason for enrolling in the first place. I was in an extended-hour academy, designed for students who already held full-time jobs. Rather than the forty-hour-a-week academy that lasted only four months, mine was a six-month, intensive evening school. To keep up with the bills while I attended, I continued to work full-time as a graveyard-shift dispatcher. Between my job, school, and care and ongoing training for my dogs, there was very little time left for anything—not even sleep.

All the recruits at the academy had cardboard placards on their desks with their names in bold letters, large enough for the instructor to read. On the front, mine said "K. Albrecht." But on the back, facing me at my desk, I had taped a picture of Rachel, my Weimaraner, and me with the letters "F.B.H." in blue magic marker alongside it. "Future Bloodhound Handler." There were many evenings when I would have put my head down on that desk and taken a long, much-needed nap had it not been for my goal sitting there, right in front of me in bright blue.

After three months of total exhaustion, I got a break. The police department in nearby Reedley, California, was one of the few that was hiring. Reedley was a small, fertile agricultural town located southeast of Fresno.

I interviewed in a competitive application process with thirty other recruits. The testing included an initial interview panel that consisted of a field training officer, a sergeant, and a lieutenant. I was asked questions about the law, my background, my character, and my ability to use good judgment. At the end of the interview, I explained my goal: to work in law enforcement as a dog handler. Reedley had a K-9 unit, and my statement was received with positive nods. Three weeks later, I accepted the job offer. They put me on salary until I finished my training, and I was mercifully able to leave my full-time job and focus my energy on doing well at the academy. I graduated on December 11, 1991; and under the supervision of a field training officer, I started pounding a beat the very next day.

As soon as I earned that badge, I was ready to go get my long-awaited bloodhound. A few weeks after graduation, I started looking for just the right puppy. I had heard there was a litter of pups in Los Gatos, a suburb of San Jose. When I called the breeder, he seemed almost surprised to have a prospective buyer on the phone, but he invited me to come and see the pups the next day.

I went, but with reservations. I knew better than to run out and buy the first puppy I saw. I'd just look these pups over to help me get a feel for what I was looking for—and what I was not looking for. And then I'd be ready to start my search for a bloodhound puppy in earnest.

As I pulled up the steep, rut-filled dirt driveway that led to the breeder's isolated home, I was greeted by the sound of bellowing howls from the older, mature bloodhounds. Bloodhounds do not bark—they practically sing. They open their mouths, shape their lips into a big Cheerio-like O, and out comes a long, drawn-out "rooooooo, rooooooo" melody.

This was the first time I had ever heard this music, and it gave me goose bumps as I approached the house.

The breeder ambled out his front door wearing a baggy black T-shirt, matching black running pants that looked an awful lot like tights, and running shoes. He was something of a wizard with bloodhounds and had a reputation for having great dog skills. He shook my hand and invited me to come and take a look at the puppies.

And there they were—three puppies and their mother in a giant dog pasture where horses had once roamed. The breeder had fenced in a large, dirt paddock and lined it with chicken wire so the dogs could not crawl out. There was straw mixed in the area to keep the mud to a minimum and give the dogs a soft place to sleep. There were several large plastic dog crates, wire crates, empty stainless-steel dog dishes, and a large watering trough. There were no cushy dog beds, no toys, no blankets, no collars—none of the things you hope to find when you go looking at puppies. The older, baying adult hounds were segregated from the younger dogs.

The yipping puppies were jumping all over each other with the mother, struggling to be the first to greet me as I approached the gate. They were four months old. All had big ears and big feet and were huge compared to the six-week-old peanut Rachel had been when I brought her home. They were too old for the kind of temperament testing I had done with Rachel. There were two boys and one girl; it was the female I was most interested in—after all, my all-girl household had worked out very well so far.

My preference didn't last long. I called the female pup over to me. She immediately jumped up and put her paws on my chest. Not good. I wanted a puppy that was submissive, not dominant. As I scratched her ears, she suddenly turned around and snapped at a male puppy that had tried to nuzzle up for some attention.

She was definitely not going to fit in at my house.

The little male had big, floppy, oar-shaped, chocolate-colored ears. His coat was the color of cinnamon, and he had a soft black, velour-like muzzle. He had enough saggy skin on his small frame to cover a Great Dane, and little brown Bambi eyes with excessive, loose skin that hung low below them. This comical droopy-eyed hangover look was normal for a bloodhound, but I had not yet spent a lot of time around these dogs, and I was charmed by the woe-is-me appearance it gave the dog.

The small male puppy had cowered from the dominant female, but he eagerly came in my direction when I called him. Even though he was a little skittish when I reached out to pet him, it only took him a minute to decide he liked me. He slumped against my leg and sighed.

And that was pretty much all it took. A cute pair of ears and a little snuggle, and all my reservations went out the window. I had wanted one of these dogs so badly, and for such a long time, that when I finally saw my opportunity to have one of my own, and he acted as though he belonged to me, I grabbed him and never looked back.

An hour after turning the corner into that backyard, I was packing my new puppy into Rachel's wire dog crate in the back of my new pickup truck. I had written a check for five hundred of his six-hundred-dollar price tag. I would send the rest out of my next paycheck. I paused for just a minute to look at my new puppy after I had him loaded in the truck. I had just jumped at the chance to pay six hundred dollars for a four-month-old dog of questionable breeding, and I couldn't get him home fast enough. This was going to be great.

It was anything but great. I named the puppy A.J., and in as many ways as Rachel had been a perfect puppy, he was not. I should have known, of course, before I even agreed to take him. A.J., bless his heart, had spent all of his days on this planet, right up until I put him in my truck, living in a horse paddock by an isolated house in the mountains. Because of that very limited experience of the world, he was afraid of everything new he encountered.

He must have been in a car once, because he had had his shots, but he didn't seem to remember. He was terrified while getting into the crate in my truck, more terrified when

I started it, a panicked wreck when it started moving, and carsick before we even got to the highway. When I arrived home three hours later, I unloaded my trembling puppy and plopped him down in my plush backyard. A.J. didn't know what to do about the grass. This was his first experience with the green stuff under his feet. When he discovered it in quantity, he was afraid to walk on it. We went through the same horrified and terrified act with each new surface A.J. discovered—first the grass, then the linoleum in the kitchen, then the carpet in my cabin.

A.J. had never spent any time inside a house. All the new sights, smells, sounds, and textures were a shock to his system. Most frightening of all, as far as he was concerned, were the two big dogs already living there. As Rachel raced up to greet the new puppy, A.J. turned around and squeezed himself headfirst into a corner.

Katie, who I figured would be jealous, made a quick assessment of the new dog's ridiculous behavior. She sniffed at A.J. with disdain, turned her back on him, and sauntered off to the couch. Like a pouting child, Katie silently conveyed her disapproval by staring at me, as if to ask, *Of all the puppies, you pick* this *one?*

That night A.J. whimpered and howled in his crate, keeping us all awake. I could hear the disapproval in Katie's sighs as she shifted around in the night, trying to ignore the unhappy puppy. Rachel seemed unfazed. I could hear her lightly snoring between A.J.'s mournful howls.

The next morning, I wrestled a collar onto A.J. and

snapped on a leash. I thought he was going to have a heart attack. The presence of the unfamiliar object around his neck, plus the tether to me, was more than he could stand. I carried him outside, set him down in the driveway, and encouraged him to follow me. He locked up all four of his feet and refused to move. I pleaded and tried to coax him with treats. He suddenly lunged forward and bolted until he hit the end of the lead in front of me and froze in place. Each time I tried to encourage him to move, A.J. would burst forward and shoot past me in panic and then freeze again at the end of the lead. He was confused and afraid. I was deeply dismayed.

The following day, I took A.J. to the veterinarian for a once-over. He was terrified from the moment we walked into the office. Once again, A.J. planted his feet and refused to move. As I tried to coax him forward, he lost control of his bladder. And as if his fearful, socially unacceptable demeanor were not enough, when we finally did get him into the office, the vet discovered that my new "baby" had fleas and a nasty ear infection.

I called the breeder in Los Gatos and told him I wanted my money back. "I'm going to have to bring him back," I explained. "He's afraid of everything. I can't even get him to walk on a leash. He won't eat, and he's terrified of my other dogs."

"No," the breeder replied matter-of-factly. "He's the right dog for you. You just need to spend more time with him. He'll learn to trust you."

I was shocked. I had expected him to tell me what time I could bring the faulty puppy back. I guess, as a remorseful buyer with a six-hundred-dollar defective purchase, I should have stood my ground. Instead, I decided to give it a little longer. Maybe A.J. did just need more time and attention. And flea medication, and ear drops, and a special diet for his nervous stomach.

For no better reason than the fact that, beyond all his fears, this puppy had a very sweet personality and was adorable in his own awkward way, I was willing to try. Since it was obvious we were not going to be conquering any training exercise—or even basic obedience—right away, I decided to start at square one with my new dog. I left the collar on but put away the leash for a few days and gave A.J. a chance to settle in on his own terms. I did my best to ignore his tearfulness and threw myself into trying to discover what would make this dog feel happy and secure.

It didn't take long to discover that A.J.'s greatest joy in life came in the form of having his chest rubbed. He was happy for a scratch on the head or a pat on the back, but once he discovered I might be persuaded to rub his chest, he started trying to find ways to weasel under my hand so I would do so. After a few days of getting used to his surroundings, A.J. started, ever so slightly, to relax.

And by then, I wouldn't have returned him to the breeder no matter what was wrong with him. He was my bloodhound, reserved and neurotic or not, and he was a part of my family.

I couldn't wait to start training A.J., and I spent a lot of my time studying and preparing for the work that would come. If

I could turn my fearful, gawky puppy into a well-trained, successful search dog, then I'd have an open door to work both dogs professionally. A.J. and I could get hired as a K-9–officer team, and my law enforcement contacts would get Rachel and me more cases as well.

The first games were very simple. I'd snap on the harness and lead, and one of my nieces or nephews would play with A.J. and then take off and hide just around the corner. A.J. would watch eagerly, and just as his playmate disappeared, I would command him to "Search!" My little hound would enthusiastically lead me to the hidden quarry.

The next step I added was the scent article. Every time someone ran away and hid, I would have them wave a T-shirt, rag, or something else they had wiped their scent on and drop it on the ground as they took off. Before giving the search command, I would walk A.J. up to the scent article on the ground and point at the item as I commanded, "Take scent." As A.J. was sniffing the item, I would release my hold on his collar and give the search command.

Soon A.J. graduated to using the scent article of choice for bloodhound handlers: a sterile gauze pad. I used sterile gauze pads to collect scent because they were bacteria-free and scent-free. Once A.J. was ready to work real cases, I would have to collect scent on gauze pads because touching or taking something from the person we wanted to trail could potentially disturb physical evidence. I could collect scent from something as obscure as a chair where the subject had been sitting or the steering wheel of a car he drove. This simple tool opened up unlimited possibilities in making sure A.J. could always have scent to start his searches.

A.J. quickly mastered the short runaway games as well as the concept of sniffing the scent article. His progress in training was better than I had expected. I began to lengthen the trails, added turns, and had my helpers hide in unusual places such as lying prone inside the back seat of a car or sitting high up in a tree. Within a month or so of starting to play hide-and-seek, A.J. could easily find a person who had hidden from him during one of these games—even the ones who had traveled a good distance and hidden well.

Most of the other bloodhound handlers I trained with taught their dogs to jump up and plant their front paws on the chest of the person they were seeking as a form of identification. I decided to create a gentler form of identification for my bloodhound: I came up with the idea to train A.J. to sit and use one paw to "push" on the leg of the person he had found. The method was almost the same as the way I had trained Katie to push on a flyball box to release a tennis ball. "Push!" was a common command in flyball racing, but it appears I might have been the first to add it to the repertoire of search-dog commands.

I was a big believer in loud verbal praise for my dogs. When A.J. found the person at the end of the trail, I would either sound off with loud, "Gooooood boooooooy, A.J." cheers or, on occasions in which he solved more difficult trails, I would sing an impromptu song that usually started with, "Hip, hip, hooray for the happy hound dog!" I did everything I could to assure that my dog learned to love his job.

Of course, we still had at least a year of advanced training ahead of us. I received this upper-level training from experienced police bloodhound handlers, most of whom were members of a bloodhound training organization called the National Police Bloodhound Association, and from a handful of expert civilian handlers in California. Once a year, I traveled to a rural camp in Grantsville, Maryland, where I attended a bloodhound seminar with other police officers. I worked A.J. on trails where the scent was several hours, even several days, old. I was assigned to a trainer and a small group of other handlers who helped put A.J. through his paces. A "trail layer" would walk into the woods and stand in one location or walk around in a small circle, leaving a heavy concentration of scent known as a "scent pool," where the scent tends to hover in the area. It was A.J.'s job to work through the large plume of scent and figure out which direction the subject went from there.

We also worked on finding a person who had walked from the woods into a business district and then waited outside a store. A.J. passed this with flying colors, ignoring passersby and honing in on his trail layer. We trained on "split trails," where two or three people walked out together and then at a designated point split apart and headed in different directions. A.J. consistently took the correct split in these trails and found and identified the right person.

After each trip, I left Maryland with a binder full of

information and a head full of new training ideas. Once at home, I added new challenges to my training program. The most important of these was to teach A.J. to work a "negative trail."

"Negative trail" training means that you teach a dog to give a clear indication when there is no scent at the start of a trail. The purpose of working negative trails is to make sure that the handler can read the dog and know what its physical signals are when it can't find the scent. As many dog handlers have learned the hard way, if you don't train your bloodhound on negative trails, then the dog will learn to sniff the article and take off at a run, whether the scent is there or not, leading the handler on a wild-goose chase.

To train on a negative trail, I would collect scent from a friend whom I confirmed had not been anywhere near the area where I planned to train A.J. I would then take A.J. to the training area and present him with the scent. I knew the person's scent was nowhere in the area, and I would allow A.J. to sniff around but not encourage him to go anywhere. As soon as he stopped casting about and gave some type of indication, I would praise him. With A.J., he would cast about, shake off, and turn around to make direct eye contact with me. Once he did this, we would drive to the friend's house, where I would take A.J. into the cloud of my friend's scent and tell him "Get to work!" and allow him to then quickly find his target and receive his reward.

We also trained on "vehicle trails" so that I could learn what A.J. would do when someone he was following climbed into a car and drove off. While some bloodhounds have been trained to follow the miniscule amount of scent left behind when a victim or suspect leaves an area in a car, A.J. was not one of these dogs. Once the heavy foot trail dissipated down to a scattered, light amount from a vehicle trail, A.J. would shake off as if he were out of scent.

We were off to a great start. I loved running behind my bloodhound. I loved to watch A.J. work with his nose just above the ground, big ears dangling, completely focused on the task at hand. I had long since decided that the backyard breeder in Los Gatos was a bit of a fortuneteller—he'd certainly been right about the potential for A.J. with me. A.J. and I were an inseparable team.

Puppy Love

Lasts Forever

A Long, Long Way

Donna Chaney

From the living-room window, I watched our fifteen-year-old son, Jay, trudge down the walk toward school. I was afraid that he might turn out into the snow-blanketed fields to hunt for his lost dog again. But he didn't. Instead he turned, waved to me, and then walked on, his shoulders sagging.

His little beagle, Cricket, was missing.

Ten days had passed since that Sunday morning when Cricket did not return from his usual early romp in the fields. Jay had worried all through Sunday school and church, and that afternoon he had roamed the countryside around our home searching for his dog. At times during those first anxious days, one or another of us would rush to the door thinking we had heard a whimper.

By now my husband, Bill, and I were sure Cricket had been taken by a hunter or struck by a car. But Jay refused to give up. One evening as I stepped outside to fill our bird feeder, I heard my son's plaintive calls drifting over the winter-blackened oaks and sycamores lining the fields near us. At last he came in, stamped the snow off his boots and said, "I know you think I'm silly, Mom, but I've been asking God about Cricket, and I keep getting the feeling that he's out there somewhere."

Tears glistened in his blue eyes. He ducked his head as he pulled off the boots.

I wanted to hold him close and tell him that he could get another dog. But I remembered too well the day four years before when we brought him his wriggling black, chocolate, and white puppy. The two of them had become inseparable. And though Cricket was supposed to sleep in the laundry room, it wasn't long before I'd find him snuggled on the foot of Jay's bed. He was such a lovable little fellow, I couldn't complain.

However, in the days since Cricket's disappearance, an unusually heavy snow had fallen. It was very cold. I felt sure that no lost pet could have survived.

Besides, I had my own worries. Bill and I had just committed ourselves to a real-estate business venture. With sky-rocketing mortgage interest rates, it was probably the worst time to enter the field. I'd often lie awake at night worrying about it. Here we were, in our late forties, having sold a thriving dry-cleaning business, stepping into perilous waters.

Jay had helped his father refurbish our new offices. Whenever he heard me express my concern, he'd glance up from his paint can, smile and say, "Don't worry, Mom, things will work out all right."

That was Jay, all right. We all attended church regularly; even so, Bill and I often wondered where Jay got his strong faith. Perhaps the blow of losing a much-loved older brother in an auto accident when he was six turned Jay to the Lord for help. In any case, I'd often find him in his room, reading the Bible, Cricket curled up at his feet.

Ten days had passed since Cricket had disappeared. I told Jay there was such a thing as carrying hope too far.

Looking out the window, he said, "I know it seems impossible, Mom, with the snow and all. But Jesus said a sparrow doesn't fall without God knowing it. And," he said, looking at the floor, "that must be true of dogs too, don't you think?"

What could I do? I hugged him and sent him off to school. Then I drove over to our real-estate office, where I forgot all about missing dogs in the bustle of typing up listings and answering the phone. The housing market seemed to be in more of a slump than ever, and mortgages were scarce. I glanced over at my husband, who was working on a financial arrangement with a forlorn young couple, and wondered if any of us would make it.

The phone rang. It was Jay.

"They let us out early today, Mom—a teacher's meeting. I thought I'd hunt for Cricket."

My heart fell.

"Jay," I said softly, trying to prepare him for the worst, "please don't put yourself through that anymore. The radio says it's only ten above zero, and you know there's little chance of . . . "

"But, Mom," he pleaded, "I have this feeling. I've got to try."

"All right," I sighed. "There's a pie I baked on the stove. Help yourself to some of it before you go."

I turned back to typing up the listings. I was so consumed by my work that it did not seem long before the afternoon sun had left our office window. I hoped Jay was back home now, watching television or doing his homework.

But he wasn't at home. Instead, he was still out hunting for Cricket.

After our phone call, he had put on his boots and taken off through the field where he and Cricket used to go. He walked about a half-mile east and then heard some dogs barking in the distance. They sounded like penned-up beagles, so he headed in that direction. Crossing a bean field, he came upon a snowmobile someone had left sitting there. He looked it over and started walking again. But now, for some reason he couldn't determine, he found himself walking away from the barking.

He came to some railroad tracks. Hearing a train coming, he decided to watch it pass. The engineer waved at him as the train roared by. With a boy's curiosity, Jay wondered if the tracks would be hot after a train went over them. So he climbed the embankment and felt them; they were cold, of course.

Now he didn't know what to do. He pitched a few rocks and finally decided to walk back down the tracks toward where he had heard the dogs barking earlier. As he stepped down the ties, the wind gusted and some hunters' shotguns echoed in the distance.

Then it happened.

Something made Jay stop dead still in his tracks. It seemed as if everything became quiet. And from down the embankment, in a tangled fencerow, came a faint sound, a kind of whimper.

Jay tumbled down the bank, his heart pounding. At the

fencerow he pushed some growth apart and there was a piti-
fully weak Cricket, dangling by his left hind foot, caught in
the rusty strands of the old fence. His front paws barely
touched the ground. The snow around him was eaten away. It
had saved him from dying of thirst.

My son carried Cricket home and phoned me ecstatically.

Stunned, I rushed to the house. In the kitchen was a very
thin Cricket lapping food from his dish with a deliriously
happy boy kneeling next to him.

Finishing his food, he looked up at Jay. In the little dog's
adoring brown eyes I saw the innocent faith that had sustained him through those arduous days, the trust that someday
his master would come.

I looked at my son, who, despite all logic, went out with
that same innocent faith and was guided to his desire. And I
knew that if Bill and I, doing the best we could, walked in that
same faith, we too would be guided through strange and cir-
cuitous paths of life, in the ways we were meant to go.

Easter Surprise

Karen Spring

"Don't worry, Karen," my mother kept telling me. "You and Eric are young and healthy. It'll happen when the time is right." I wanted to believe that, but my husband and I had been trying to have a baby for almost a year. Our failure to conceive was all I could think about.

One Saturday afternoon in October, I went for a walk around the neighborhood to clear my mind. A group of women with baby carriages were at the corner chatting. I could hear sweet gurgles coming from their strollers. I waved to the mothers, but inside I wanted to cry. *Please, Lord, all I want is a little one to love. When will it be my turn?* I walked back home. The tears started falling as soon as I closed the door.

"Honey, what's the matter?" Eric asked.

"Nothing. It's just . . . everyone else has babies. What's wrong with us?"

"It's going to happen. We just need to relax. It hasn't even been a year yet." He gave me a hug. But by Christmastime we were getting anxious. So I had some tests done. Everything came back clear.

Since I worked from home, my mother suggested I get a dog to keep me company. Eric thought a puppy would take my

160

mind off the baby issue. *I was a little reluctant. Do they really think a dog is going to make up for not having a baby? Besides, a puppy would chew up our new furniture.* Nevertheless, Eric convinced me to go to the animal shelter.

"What kind of dog do you guys want?" the animal shelter officer asked us.

"Beagle," I said at the same time my husband declared, "Jack Russell terrier." Eric compromised, "A puppy of some kind." The officer led us to a cage. Two puppies were scampering around.

"Are they male or female?" I asked.

"They're boys," she answered.

"If we get a dog, I want it to be a girl. They're more docile," I said.

"Wait, there's another one," the officer said. Huddled in the corner of the cage was a trembling, pumpkin-colored puppy. "It's a girl."

"What breed is she?" Eric asked.

"A beagle-terrier mix," the officer answered. We laughed. She was ours.

We took her home and named her Jade. Before long it was hard for me to imagine life without her. She followed me from room to room. When I worked in my study she'd lay her little head on my feet and take a nap. In the afternoons I'd take her for walks around the neighborhood, and I didn't feel so alone anymore.

Sure, sometimes she would get into things. "Jade, what are you doing?" I'd ask after catching her gnawing on our wing-back chair. She'd sit down at my feet and drop her head, like she was asking for forgiveness. I couldn't resist picking her up and kissing her. "It's okay, Jade. I still love you."

In December we took Jade to the mall and had her picture taken with Santa. I knew it was silly, but I wanted a Christmas photo of our little angel to put up on the fridge. *Maybe she's the only baby we're going to have*, I thought.

We were coming up on two years of trying to conceive and failing. We went to a fertility specialist and had more tests done. A few days later the doctor called. The problem wasn't with me. It was Eric. I just stood there with the receiver in my hand. Jade looked up at me from her spot at my feet, cocking her head quizzically. "I have to call Daddy," I said. I told Eric what the doctor said.

"So I'm the reason we can't have a baby," he said, his voice breaking.

"Hey, stop it. We're in this together." I tried to be strong for him. But after I hung up, I couldn't hold back my tears. Jade knew what I needed. She jumped up on my lap and licked my face.

Eric and I found out that in vitro fertilization was our only option if we were going to have a child. We wanted to give it a try before we looked into adoption. So that spring I started a painful three-shots-a-day regimen to stimulate my ovaries.

I don't know who was more nervous about the shots, me or Eric, who needed to administer them. Lying on my side that first time, I took in a deep breath, closed my eyes, and tried to relax. Still, my body tensed at the thought of the needle. Suddenly I felt something cold and wet in my hand. I opened my eyes, Jade was nudging me with her nose, as if to say, *It's okay, I'm here.* I stroked her ears, looked into her eyes, and said a quick prayer as Eric injected my thigh. A few weeks later the doctor transferred three embryos into my uterus.

"Our baby could be growing inside you," Eric said on the way home.

"I know. Wouldn't it be amazing to surprise my mom with the news at Easter dinner?"

I was getting giddy just talking about it. Then we got home to find Jade throwing up. She had eaten something she shouldn't have. Normally she'd get over it within a few hours. This time Jade wouldn't stop whimpering and heaving. We took her to the animal clinic, and they immediately admitted her for tests.

At home I couldn't concentrate. I wandered around the house. It seemed so empty without Jade scampering about.

I looked at her picture on the fridge. On the calendar underneath her photo in big red letters the words "Doctor Appointment . . . Baby?" were written in for the next day. *Tomorrow I'm going to find out if I'm pregnant.* I had forgotten all about it because I was so worried about what was wrong with Jade.

Then an awful thought struck me. *God, do I have to lose Jade to have a baby? She's my little angel—please don't take her away from me.* The next day the vet called. They'd done an ultrasound and found something lodged in Jade's intestine.

Jade ended up having surgery at the same time I was taking a blood test. After we got home from my appointment all I could think about was my sweet little puppy. *Is she going to be okay? What would I do without her?*

The phone rang and I lunged for it. "Karen, it's positive! You're pregnant."

Soon we heard from the vet. Jade had made it through her operation. The vet had removed a strip of towel from her intestine—she must have been playing with it and swallowed it.

It was a joyous Easter dinner at my mother's. Tiny votives surrounding a beautiful white-lily centerpiece cast a golden haze in the air. Eric stood up and raised his glass. "I'd like to make a toast. To my wife, who I know will always be there for me, through the good times and the bad. Who in nine months will make me a dad."

Mom squeezed my hand. She had told me things would happen when the time was right. When better than Easter to celebrate new life, to remember that God answers our prayers in ways far beyond what we imagine?

Monday we went to get Jade. As soon as she saw us, her tail started wagging. Mindful of her stitches, I gently picked her up and kissed her head. I felt blessed to have this little angel to love. And I felt even more blessed a few days later, when Eric and I found out that in nine months we would be having not one but two babies.

Caesar, Brutus, and St. Francis

Sue Monk Kidd

I'm taking you guys to church, so please try to behave, okay?" Our two rambunctious young beagles, Caesar and Brutus, sat on the front seat of the car and ignored me, their floppy ears perked to attention as they watched the stream of traffic. At the stoplight, I braked as a woman walked her black poodle across the street. Caesar and Brutus let out a string of "woo-woo-woof's."

"Now see? That's what I mean," I told them. "None of that."

It was a balmy October afternoon and we were on our way to a "Blessing of the Animals" service at Grace Episcopal Church. I'd never attended one of these services, and frankly, I had no idea what to expect. I only knew it was held each year on St. Francis Day (since St. Francis had a special love for animals) and that folks were invited to bring their pets. From the moment I'd read about it, I'd had a nudging feeling I should go.

Now I wondered if I was out of my mind. What if Caesar and Brutus disrupted the service? It would be just like them. Beagles are bred to do three things: sniff, bark and charge at anything furry. Once my son found Caesar in our fenced back-yard stranded up in a crepe myrtle tree where he'd climbed after a squirrel.

Earlier in the day I'd asked my children if they would like to come along to see the dogs blessed. "Let me get this straight," said Bob. "You're taking our dogs to church to get blessed with a lot of other animals?" He was biting the inside of his mouth to keep from laughing. Ann had simply gazed at me with her when-are-you-checking-into-the-asylum look.

I looked at the dogs, thumping their tails on the car seat, barking at everything that moved outside the car. "Will you be quiet?" I cried. The truth is, I'd never taken to these two hyperactive beagles the way I had to our beloved old, slow-moving spaniel, Captain. He'd presided quietly over the house for thirteen years before he died. These two were his so-called "replacements." Some replacements.

I turned into the church parking lot just as the service was about to begin. Beside the children's playground was a table draped in white with a St. Francis statue on it. A little crescent of children, adults, dogs—quiet dogs—and other animals had formed around it. I lashed Caesar's and Brutus's leashes to my wrists like a rodeo cowboy getting ready to ride into the ring.

The dogs came out of the car in a yapping frenzy, noses to the ground, dragging me behind them. I tugged and wrestled them over to the other animals. The priest was saying something about celebrating the presence of animals on earth, how they too were part of God's wonderful plan.

166

"Woo-woo-woof! Woo-woo-woof!" they barked and bayed at the other dogs, drowning out the voice of the priest. People looked at me and smiled sympathetically. Even the other dogs stared at me.

Caesar and Brutus then spotted a pet carrier on the ground to my left. Sitting regally behind the wire was a cat. "Woo-woo-woof!" They lunged toward the cat, nearly tipping me over. The priest was practically shouting now. I frantically tried to hush them as they strained on their leashes, which were cutting into my wrists to the point of pain. *Lord, what a disaster!* I thought. *My children were right. This was a dumb idea. Just wait till I get you two home.* I wanted to leave, but something—I don't know what—held me there.

The priest moved from one animal to the next, patting their heads, saying something to each one. Finally he stopped in front of my two disturbers of the peace and asked their names. "Caesar and Brutus," I replied in the most apologetic tone possible.

He touched their heads and smiled. "Bless you, Caesar and Brutus. We're thankful for your enthusiasm about life and for the joyful noise you make in response to it. May God watch over you and protect you."

Next we read in unison the famous prayer of St. Francis, our words filtering through the aria of my dogs' unending barking: "Lord, make me an instrument of thy peace. . . ."

Finally, mercifully, it was over.

Back home I opened the gate, let Caesar and Brutus into the backyard, then trudged into the kitchen, muttering.

"What happened?" asked my husband, Sandy.

"Those fool dogs practically ruined the St. Francis Day service. They acted like animals."

"They are animals," he pointed out.

For days I refused to let them in the house, where they usually slept. I scolded them for the least thing: for the limbs they dragged onto the deck, for turning over my Boston fern, for scratching at the door, but mostly for barking. They responded by wagging their tails and dropping a ball in front of me, hoping I would toss it. I would not.

Five days after the St. Francis Day disaster, I happened to glance out the window and see the neighbor's cat sashaying along the back fence. An eerie feeling came over me. Why weren't the dogs barking? I stepped into the yard, into an awful, empty silence. With a thudding heart I peered at the gate. It was hanging open. Caesar and Brutus were gone.

I ran down the driveway, remembering Sandy's caution to keep the gate closed. "If those two dogs ever get out, I'm afraid they'll be long gone," he'd said. Had the meter reader come through it and left it ajar? Had the wind blown it open?

I hurried along the street calling their names. After scouring the neighborhood for two hours, I came home. There had been no sign of them. They had probably seen a squirrel and tracked it clear to North Carolina by now.

Sandy came home during lunch and we drove all over town. "If we ever find them, I'll never fuss at them again," I told Sandy.

He smiled at me. "I know."

After school the children joined the search. Late into the afternoon I kept stopping people on the street. "Have you seen two little beagles?" They all shook their heads.

As the day softened into dusk, we gave up and went home. I passed their empty dog bowls in the kitchen and walked into my study. I sat alone in the shadows and traced my finger along the edge of my desk. Suddenly I remembered how the priest put his hands on their heads. What had he said? "Bless you, Caesar and Brutus. We're thankful for your enthusiasm for life. . . . May God watch over you and protect you." I laid my head down and cried.

When I dried my eyes, it was dark out. I stood at the window and wondered if we would ever see them again. Just then a part of St. Francis's prayer came floating back into my head: "Where there is doubt, let me sow faith; where there is despair, hope . . ." The words seemed full of urgency. I grabbed a flashlight and both dog leashes, and I headed out the door. "Where are you going?" Sandy asked.

"To sow faith and hope," I said.

I walked along the street, on and on, block after block.

"Woo-woo-woof!"

I froze. I would know that sound anywhere. I listened, following it until I came upon Caesar and Brutus sniffing through the garden in a stranger's yard. In the middle of the garden was a statue of St. Francis. Somehow I was not surprised.

As the dogs bounded into my arms and licked my face, I thanked God for St. Francis, who loved all creatures great and small, and who was still teaching folks today to do the same. I thanked God for blessing my two beagles and for watching over them.

Back home I gave both dogs some milk and let them curl up on the foot of my bed. I rubbed their ears, feeling that great and piercing awareness that breaks in upon us at certain times in life, the awareness of not realizing how much you love the people or things close to you until you almost lose them.

I was suddenly filled with the need to seize every day and sow it full of all those wonderful things St. Francis prayed about: love and pardon, faith and hope, light and joy.

Sandy and the children appeared at the bedroom door. I went and put my arms around them. "I don't tell you enough," I said, "but I love you."

From the foot of the bed came a resounding "Woo-woo-woof."

Ruby, Where Are You?

Hayes Beachum

I didn't feel much like having a party, but up at the house they were getting ready for my eightieth birthday. I stood gloomily in the yard watching my son, Wayne, play with the dog, the only one left from the English-shepherd business I'd let fade out two years earlier.

In my honor, Wayne and his wife, Geneva, my two daughters and their husbands, all the grandchildren, and even some of my brothers and sisters had gathered. But why celebrate? What was the point of their spending time with a dismal old stick-in-the-mud like me?

Wayne gave the dog a final pat and turned to me. "Why not breed her again, Dad?"

I started fussing with the latch on the dog lot. "It's a shame not to," I said. "But ever since Ruby disappeared, I don't have it in me to raise a litter of pups." And that was the truth of it.

Wayne's arm slid across my shoulders. "I understand, Dad. The whole family loved that dog. . . ." His voice trailed off and he changed the subject. "Let's get up to the house. Must be close to party time."

I trudged along with Wayne, trying to swallow the lump

171

that still rose up in my throat every time I thought of Ruby. She'd come into my life after I'd sold my service station and retired. Well, not exactly retired.

"I refuse to just sit in that rocking chair on the porch," I'd told my wife, Estelle.

After fifty-five years of being married to me, she knew I needed to be busy with something, and she'd nodded. "Ask the Lord about it. He and you will come up with something. Always have."

I prayed about it, and after a while, in one of the farm magazines, I came across an article on English shepherds. It explained what good working dogs they are and how you could start a profitable part-time business with them. So I'd bought a couple of dogs, and before long people were waiting in line to buy the puppies as soon as they were weaned.

It was productive work, it paid fairly well, and it kept me busy. But I was careful not to become personally attached to the dogs. I hadn't had time for a dog of my own before and it was too late in life to "have" a dog now. That was for young boys. So mainly the puppies came and went. I took good care of them, fed them well, and exercised them, but that was all.

Until Ruby. I knew from the moment I saw that pup that there was something different about her. It wasn't just the soft puppy fur that hinted of a shiny sable coat to come, or the snowy white bib and collar. It wasn't her gentle, lovable nature. All the other dogs had those same features. No, there was something special about her eyes, a searching gaze that reached clear through the all-business attitude I'd kept with the other dogs.

Ruby grew quickly, and before I knew it, she was begging to be let outside the lot. But instead of scampering across the yard like the rest of the youngsters, she stuck at my heels, following me as I did the chores. It wasn't long until she started jumping up onto the seat beside me in the pickup and riding out to the old family farm, where I still kept a few cattle. She'd help round them up, then sit down beside me while we watched them munch the hay we'd brought.

The day I'd had my heart attack out there at the farm, she'd stayed right by my side, licking my face and whining me back to consciousness. I'd finally managed to get a grip on her collar, and together we'd made it back to the pickup. She sat close beside me in her usual seat as we crawled the truck back home in low gear.

After that she was as much a part of me as my right arm. As she got older, I taught her a few special tricks. I'd hold out a stick and she'd jump over it, or I'd form a circle with my arms and she'd jump through. But it was her own idea to go ahead of me into the fields and flush out snakes. How long had she done that? Nine or ten years, as long as I'd had her. Or maybe it'd be better to say "as long as she'd had me."

That day I came home from church and found her gone, I thought I'd just forgotten to close the gate and she'd surely show up by supper. But she didn't come back. I spent days, weeks, driving up and down back roads and highways, looking for any sign of her. I advertised on the radio and in the newspapers. But nothing helped. She was gone.

"Don't give up," Estelle kept telling me. "The Bible says

'in due season we shall reap, if we faint not' [Galatians 6:9]. Where's your faith, anyway?"

Where indeed? The fact of the matter is, I was losing it. And a lot of other things changed after that. I didn't have the gumption to raise dogs anymore. Days that had once been spent following Ruby across the fields seemed to drag. I tried to call up the drive that had carried me through some mighty tough years, but it seemed to be gone. So I began to feel sorry for myself and stray far from the good Lord, whom I'd always trusted.

At the house everybody acted excited about my birthday, but I couldn't help but say to myself, *Why are they all here?* I knew the youngsters would rather be with their friends. And if my son and daughters would admit it, there were probably other things they'd prefer doing. After all, I was just someone they had to come and visit, someone not much good to anyone anymore.

We got through lunch, then went outside to cut the cake Estelle had baked. I made an effort to act like always, declaring that the grandchildren would have to help me blow out the candles and joking about how there was enough fire there to keep warm during a blizzard. Later I sat out on the porch in that rocking chair I swore I'd never use, faking a nap, while my grandson, Charles, cleaned his rifle and the ladyfolk searched the flower beds for early bloomers.

Gradually I found myself watching my granddaughters, Shearra and Beth, as they tried to shoo away an old stray dog, coat dusty and matted, that kept wandering into the yard. As I watched, Estelle joined them. The harder they tried to scare off the dog, the more determined it was to stay. Just when they'd think it was gone, the mutt would reappear, sneaking under the bushes or around the back of the house.

"Come on," I heard Wayne say to Geneva, "let's go help Grandma and the girls."

The five of them played hide-and-seek with the old dog for a while, then quite suddenly Wayne and Geneva stopped chasing and stood off to the side talking. Before I knew it, the whole family seemed to be whispering.

"What's the matter with them anyway?" I asked myself, and I got up for a better look.

They were all staring at that stray dog. The poor animal was in even worse shape than I had thought at first. Its hair was coming out in patches, and the coat looked like one giant cocklebur. The old fella must have been out in the fields for months.

"Dad . . ." Wayne spoke softly. "Dad, come on over here. . . ." Geneva picked up a stick and held it out a foot or two from the ground. The stray saw it, moved toward it, studied it for a moment, then sat down before it.

I moved closer. A twig snapped under my boot, and the dog turned and stared up at me. Its eyes were soft, velvet, and its gaze . . . its gaze . . . it was a searching gaze that went right through to the heart of me. The dog turned and, moving as if in slow motion, jumped smoothly over the stick.

My control was beginning to crumble. I was almost scared to hope. Yet I had to know for sure. I formed my arms into a circle and waited, afraid even to look.

But a nudge against my leg forced me to look into the velvet eyes again. Then with what seemed barely an effort, Ruby leapt through the circle, her matted fur grazing my arms.

All at once everyone was shouting and crying and hugging. There was no doubt! Ruby had come back!

I dropped down beside Ruby on the grass and pulled her onto my lap. "Whoever stole her must have taken her a long way away," Wayne exclaimed. "Wonder how far she traveled?" I took a rough paw in my hand and examined the worn pad, marveling at the courage it must have taken her to get back home, the determination, the persistence.

The thought then came streaking into my head: Ruby hadn't given up. But I had. I had given up on life—on the blessings that were all around me, even on the faith that told me clearly to keep on and not be faint.

"What's happened to this party?" I shouted. "Let's keep this party going. After all, it isn't every day a man celebrates his eightieth birthday!"

I got to my feet and slipped my arms around Beth and Shearra as we walked back toward the house with Ruby twining in and out of our legs.

Search for a
Lost Dog

Harvey Scott

One frigid December morning, I bundled up, grabbed my keys, and stepped outside. Godshaux, my six-year-old Australian shepherd, excitedly circled around by the truck while I warmed the engine. Then he raced my old four-wheel drive to the mailbox near the highway.

We were good together, Godshaux and I—we were both independent types. It was just the two of us living in my twenty-three-foot trailer amid a wooded valley near the rugged Selkirk Mountains of northern Idaho. I survived without running water, commercial electricity, telephone and many other things most would consider necessities. But I had Godshaux, and his companionship was about all I needed.

He ran the half mile easily, kicking up clods of snow. Just before the roadbed he stopped, spun twice as was his custom, then lined up south with the snowmobile path that followed the grade. He stretched out quickly to full stride and kept up with me going twenty-five miles an hour along the highway that paralleled his path. Then he was lost from my sight as a wall of young jack pine came between us. We had made this run most mornings for six years, ever since Godshaux was a pup. For the last four of those years, he had been blind.

Driving the twenty miles to town for supplies, I marveled at the way the dog had adjusted. One eye had turned moony from cataracts, the other had soon failed. But this sightless fellow had learned to run through the timber, chase a cat, and catch about three yellow jackets out of ten. A sighted dog couldn't do much better.

The closest I came to understanding his predicament was comparing how, as a kid, I played piano by ear in the old church where Dad preached his fire-and-brimstone sermons. I felt my way around the keys, sensing the combinations of notes, almost as if my fingers knew where to go. I pictured God guiding my hands along.

It had been a long time since I'd let him guide me. Dad liked to quote in a booming voice, "The Lord is my rock and my fortress." I was taught to depend on God for everything. But as I grew up, I relied more and more on myself instead.

When I returned from town that morning, Godshaux was not at lane's end to meet me. He always met me when I returned.

Godshaux was in trouble.

I went to the railroad grade to track him. He had navigated by scent marks, beacons left from countless trips. He grew careless, though; he had crossed the boundary of his mental map, the blacktop lake road now covered with a carpet of snow.

I followed his tracks down the short, steep bank on the

other side of the road, where he had circled, realizing his mistake. He had gone back across the road to search out his trail and had missed it by just ten feet. Here I ran out of tracks. I checked both sides of the road for another mile, but I found not one sign in the snowbanks.

That night the temperature stood at zero. As I climbed into bed, I imagined Godshaux wandering the snow-choked roads, searching for a familiar sound or smell as he strayed farther and farther from home. He would be easy prey for the coyotes.

But what could I do? I needed Godshaux—and he needed me. *The Lord is my rock and my fortress,* spoke a familiar voice in my head. Then instinct took over, just as it had when I played piano. For the first time in ages I prayed, and prayed with a vengeance, as Dad had done. Rattling the gates, he called it. "God, have mercy on my friend, who has never been disobedient to me. And be with me," I added, "though I have strayed from you."

One harsh storm followed another. By the third day I could not eat. Trips to the mailbox were torture without that old faithful muzzle nibbling my hand.

In the mornings, before daylight, I patrolled the roads. At the least sound in the night, I threw open the door and probed the darkness with the beam of my flashlight. At week's end I struggled to accept what I knew was true: Godshaux was never coming home. "I depend on you," I said, looking up at the clear sky, "whatever your will."

Late on the eighth day, my neighbor brought a message.

A woman believed she had seen Godshaux. I harnessed my hope and went to meet her.

"Down the road just through the gate on the snowbank," she said, pointing west. As I drove slowly I saw that the tracks were thick. Many were bloodstained. Sharp ice and barbed wire lay hidden in the high snowbanks. A battle raged inside me. Everything within me wanted it to be him. Logic told me that it couldn't be so. In my mind, I had buried him.

I got out of my truck and eased through the gate. I stopped. The dog raised his head. "Godshaux!" His ears lifted. He cocked his head. It was what he must have been listening for these past eight days. He knew my voice, as God had known mine.

Godshaux jumped into my arms, squealing his greeting, a sound he had never made before. He didn't know it, but a miracle had happened. Dogs don't know of miracles, but there are people who know.

I know.

Down the Mineshaft

Don "Booty" Hall

Pistol, my three-year-old beagle, ran to me, tail going like crazy, as soon as I walked in the door that Saturday last December. I gave him a pat on the head and grabbed the ringing phone. *What now?* I was having one of those weeks when nothing seemed to go right, not at work, not at home. Ever since my divorce, I'd had spells like that every now and then—times when it felt almost as if the Lord had forgotten about me.

My ex-wife was on the other end of the line. "I'm sorry, Don, I know I told you Kyle and Kasey could spend Christmas with you, but I can't get them to you till New Year's."

Much as I wanted to have the boys with me for Christmas, I was too worn out to raise a fuss. "Well, Pistol," I said after I'd hung up, "looks like it's you and me this Christmas. At least we got some fun planned tomorrow." We were going rabbit hunting with my cousins and their dogs. From the way Pistol barked, it seemed as if he understood every word I'd said. For all I knew, he did. Pistol is one smart dog.

The next morning I met Vernon, Bruce and Greg at the top of an abandoned mining strip about ten miles south of Wheelwright. The air was cool and humid—just right for a dog to pick up a scent. Pistol bounded out of my truck and onto the grassy slope. Half the fun of hunting came from watching Pistol work a field, somehow knowing just what I wanted him to do. We moved down the hill, the dogs' white-tipped tails zigzagging through the grass in front of us. I could feel my mood lifting. Maybe this wasn't going to be one of those low times after all.

We'd gone half a mile when I realized I hadn't seen Pistol for a while. Usually he checked in with me every couple of minutes, running back from the pack with a wag of his tail.

"You seen Pistol?" I asked Vernon.

"Not for a while, now that you mention it," he said.

"It's not like him to take off. We better look for him." We rounded the other dogs into the truck and set off down the gentle slope again, calling out for Pistol.

"Hold up," said Vernon. "I heard a bark. Behind us."

I saw a foot-wide hole in the ground. A mine break. My heart sank. Mine breaks are deep cracks in the earth created from dynamiting in the mineshafts. I dropped to my knees and called into the hole. "Pistol! Are you down there, boy?" A faint bark came back from the darkness. A mine break could go down three or four hundred feet, clear to the mineshaft itself. The opening to this one was narrow, too narrow for even a wiry kid like one of my boys. I couldn't see more than a couple of feet down. This was bad trouble.

What to do? I paced. I fretted. Time and again, I called out to Pistol, then reminded myself not to get him excited. The more I studied the hole, the worse the situation looked. I lowered a rope, hoping Pistol would grab on. He did, but he let go before I could pull him up. The break was so small and the walls were so jagged, I couldn't imagine how I would ever get him out.

"Go home and get some rest, Don," Vernon finally said as the sun dropped behind the trees. "We'll think of something tomorrow. He'll be okay."

"Don't worry, boy," I called to my dog. "I'll be back for you." Pistol barked back as if to say, *I know you will.*

I hardly slept a wink. Since the divorce, Pistol had been my only steady company, the one soul who was always happy to see me and who never failed to bring me up if I was down. *Lord, I know my dog's counting on me,* I prayed. *What good am I if I can't save him?*

On the way to the mine break the next morning—Monday—I stopped and talked to my friend Carol, Pistol's vet. She made some calls, then met Vernon and me with a length of rope with a net attached to the end. Nope. The hole was just too dark, too narrow and too deep. That afternoon a local TV crew showed up. "Are you sure you want to put this on TV?" I asked the reporter. "What if Pistol doesn't make it out?"

"The more people that hear about this," the reporter said, "the better the chances he will get out. Folks will want to help."

That night I dumped a coffee can of dog food down the hole, hoping some of it would reach Pistol. *Lord, let Pistol understand that I haven't given up on him.*

"Look, Don," Vernon said, "we're not giving up. But maybe you should prepare yourself for the worst." All that night in my sleep, I heard Pistol's barks.

Tuesday and Wednesday held more of the same. I lowered

a feed sack with some more dog kibble in it. Even if the food was getting to Pistol, he had to be weak from dehydration. And there was no telling if the fall had hurt him. By Thursday his barks had faded to distant whimpers. *Lord, I've been doubting you some lately. Now I'm going to just put my faith in you. Save my dog.*

Thursday night I stopped by the vet's. "Pikeville City Fire and Rescue has one of those sewer cams—a cable with a camera at the end of it," Carol said. "I'll ask if they can bring it to the break tomorrow."

The mayor of Pikeville phoned me that night. "I know how much a good dog means to a man, Don. I'm sending our full rescue squad."

The next morning six men in rescue uniforms were waiting at the hill. One carried a long metal hose coiled over his shoulder with a big eye at the end—the sewer cam. Foot by foot, they lowered it into the break.

"Okay," the cameraman said. "Looks like we're about two feet off the bottom."

I stared at the monitor. I could see the jagged rock walls and a stretch of flat ground where the break opened up.

"What do we do now?" I asked.

"Wait," the cameraman said.

Five minutes went by. Then ten. Then twenty. *Come on, Pistol. Come on, boy.* What if he was too weak to move?

"There he is!"

Pistol walked right past the camera. He was still alive! *But what now?*

The cameraman grabbed a length of nylon line and

fashioned one end into a loop. He lowered it until the loop hung right below the camera. "If your dog sticks his head in," he said, "I'm going to pull him up fast, before he chokes."

Not a bad idea. But what were the chances that Pistol would walk over and just stick his head through? I thought of all those times out in the field when Pistol seemed to read my mind. *Lord, if you're listening, lead Pistol over to that rope. Tell him what I want.*

I couldn't believe it . . . Pistol came into view again! He looked right into the camera. *Come on, boy. Put your head through.*

Pistol hesitated a moment, his whiskers twitching. He sniffed the loop. Then he stuck his head through it.

Instantly the rescue worker yanked up. "I've got him! I've got him!" In a moment Pistol—shivering, thin and almost too weak to stand—was in my arms, licking my face and whimpering with joy.

Christmas last year turned out pretty good after all. I had my dog back, and my faith. No, the Lord didn't forget me at all. He never does.

How to Raise
a Dog

Jack Alan

Dog owners, arise! Too long has the actual head of your family not even paid an income tax. Too long have you tried to conceal from your dog the fact that he really owns you. Too long have you searched in vain for the counsel you so sorely need when, panting and tongue hanging out, you fall back into the nearest chair and finally admit to yourself that the lively little fellow isn't going to sit up and beg, hasn't the slightest intention of leaving that frayed end of the tapestry alone, and is unshakably convinced that the mathematical center of the living-room rug is the comfort station supreme.

You can expect no help from dog books or dog doctors. In this all-important emergency, all they do is back away, muttering incoherent statements about training and psychology. And you are left holding the bag, one end of which has already been chewed away, like everything else you own.

I am no expert. I might as well tell you right now that I generally go to sleep with a large, greasy bone under my pillow because I have failed to sway my dog in his opinion that there isn't a better spot in town for bone hiding. My house is thoroughly dog-broken. But I do not intend to leave my fellow man with his dog having the upper paw in the household.

I believe my predicament to be an average one, a valuable case history. I will show you how I deal with my dog. Maybe you will be able to discover where along the line something went terribly, terribly wrong.

Things started badly when I bought him. I didn't select him, he selected me. When I went to the kennel, I had decided definitely against buying four or five puppies, as I wanted to do. Phyllis claims that this is too many for a small apartment. Cunningly, however, I planned to get around this by getting as much dog as possible for my money—a Great Dane.

I looked critically at the batch of puppies, which, while only three months old, were the size of Airedales. Then one detached himself from the mob. He had a lot of filling out to do. He took, I noticed, several steps before his skin started moving along with him. He galloped over, sat down heavily on my feet, and looked me over carefully. I couldn't move, so I had to look at him too. He was obviously admiring me. His next step was to take my trouser leg in his mouth and shake it, possibly to test the quality of the material. Then he gave several pleased body wiggles, attempted to climb up on me, and washed my hand thoroughly with a salmon-pink tongue. Then he sat down again on my feet and admired me some more.

I had been chosen.

Several months have passed, and we have learned much about each other. Neither of us regrets his choice, although my training methods seem to lack something.

I have found that the very first step must be to gain his confidence. To accomplish this, I sit on the floor next to him and say, "Good little dog!" This is a flat lie and he knows it, being well aware that he is neither little nor good. He backs away several feet, presses himself close to the floor, and turns up his eyes at me with a wary "You-are-up-to-something-tricky-and-I'm-not-going-to-like-it" expression.

I reach out reassuringly and pat his nearest paw. He withdraws the paw and licks it off fastidiously.

I attempt now to get his attention by cupping both hands and saying coyly: "Guess what I've got here?"

Showing signs of interest, he nuzzles into my hands. I am caught flat-footed with nothing in them. I run to get a dog biscuit to absolve myself.

Meanwhile he stalks off bitterly to a corner of the room, tenses his forelegs, digs a hole in the carpet, and lies down in it.

I now change my approach, deciding to try the "great big playmate" tactic. Crouching on all fours, I advance on him, barking several times with mock ferocity. He decides to humor me by pretending he thinks I'm a huge, dangerous dog. With a happy yelp, he flashes around a chair and dashes upon me from behind. Since he weighs roughly eighty-two pounds at the moment, I am now flat on the floor with him on top of me. He wants to pretend he is shaking me by the neck. This is too difficult unless he actually does shake me by the back of the neck. So he does.

I get up and brush myself off. I brush *him* off me too, several times. I have now succeeded in gaining his confidence and showing him that I am a regular fellow who doesn't mind a good, clean romp, so I am through. But he isn't. He likes it too well to quit. He gets my tie in his teeth and hangs from it. It is some time before I get my breath.

He still refuses to stop. It is therefore time for me to punish him. I decide to lock him in the bathroom. This consists of the following steps:

1. He instantly senses my purpose and scrambles into the bedroom and under the bed.
2. I rush after him and say, "Come out from under there this minute!"
3. He doesn't.
4. I get down on the floor and look under the bed. We face each other. I blink, which gives him the round.
5. I mutter several dire threats. So does he.
6. I hold out my handkerchief, hoping he will grab it and pull, thereby enabling me to drag him out.
7. He grabs it and pulls.
8. We are now both under the bed.
9. I seize him firmly and wriggle out.
10. A head bumps severely against the box spring. It is not his.

11. I shove and pull him into the bathroom and back out, closing the door.

12. I stop closing the door to avoid catching his nose in it.

13. I shove him back and close the door, catching my hand in it.

14. We both howl simultaneously.

Returning to the living room, tired but victorious (look up Pyrrhic in any good encyclopedia), I now proceed to describe my dog to you. He is still a puppy, seven months old. He is a good dog to have for a case history because, although a thoroughbred, he has a character which is practically a cross section of that of America's dogs.

Although large and getting larger, it is his opinion that he is a lap dog and as such entitled to climb on my chair whether I am in it or not. When I can catch him to give him a bath, he emerges as a dull gold in color with a mouth fringed with black. This mouth is already large enough to contain my arm and, when I am giving him a bath, does. Like all his breed, he has a short coat, but he sheds it with the success of the collie. He has a way of searching out tidbits in his food which probably reveals that in spite of his pedigree he contains a trace of anteater. He has a beery sort of baritone. And he is very democratic in his ideas about love.

When I first got him I called him Gilbert, the name I still introduce him by. The only word he will always answer to, however, is Food, so I generally call him that.

Food, or Gilbert, is still in the bathroom, you will recall. This is my golden opportunity to get something to eat unbeknownst to him. Let me explain.

Since I have known Gilbert, I have had few square meals at home. This is because Gilbert is adept at a quiet, effective sort of bullying. When I am eating, he is too wily to use strong-arm tactics, realizing that force will be answered with force. He therefore just looks at me tragically. He keeps looking at me. He meditates on man's inhumanity to dog. He sighs. Beginning to feel like a heartless gourmand, I transfer my little morsel of food to my mouth. His glance never wavers. He drools slowly.

As a result, I spend a large part of my time at my dinner table chewing things up a little for Gilbert. Then I give them to him, cursing.

But now that Gilbert is in the bathroom, I turn on the radio full blast and enter the kitchen singing loudly, hoping that both noises will distract him.

It is a losing game. Gilbert, who would sleep soundly through a collision with another planet, easily detects the noiseless opening of the electric icebox. No sooner do I reach a guilty hand to a roast-beef bone than Gilbert utters a series of agonized cries, giving the entire neighborhood the impression that I am murdering him by inches. In self-defense I rush to the bathroom to make him stop.

He is very happy as I open the door, particularly since a well-timed move enables him to snatch the beef bone from my hand and rush back to the bathroom.

I am about to follow him to get back my bone when the doorbell rings.

It is Mrs. Garble, a middle-aged woman I do not like. She is the president of Phyllis' club. She is also a cat lover. She expresses relief at being able to come in for once and not have that great brute of a dog jumping all over her. Looking nervously, she asks where he is. I tell her.

"What in the world is he doing in the bathroom?" she says.

"Well, really, Mrs. Garble," I reply primly, "he *said* he wanted to wash his hands."

This keeps her quiet for a moment. It then develops that she wants to see Phyllis, who isn't home. She looks at the carpet, which has no more than a normal amount of Gilbert's hair on it.

"Goodness gracious!" she says, clucking, "I don't see how you can keep a Great Dane in a city apartment! Why, I'd just as soon keep a horse in one!"

I bristle and stifle a desire to say, "Oh, so you don't think I ought to keep my horse, either?"

Gilbert chooses this moment to enter. And not, to my surprise, with his usual attitude, which practically says, "Oh my chin and whiskers! What wonderful things have I been missing!" Instead, he comes in with measured dignity. He casts a sedate glance at Mrs. Garble.

"He seems to be getting much better manners," she says grudgingly. "You certainly are training him to behave like a gentleman!"

I decide that Mrs. Garble, too, seems to be getting better manners. I warm toward her, as I do to all types of characters who have a kind word to say for Gilbert. I even toy with the idea of giving her a drink.

I watch with paternal pride as Gilbert walks slowly over to her. He sniffs at her leg in a genteel way. I beam reassuringly. Mrs. Garble smiles back uncertainly. Gilbert seems about to walk past her. He doesn't. He stops. Trained to observe such matters, I suddenly notice an uncertain attitude, a slight quivering of the muscles of Gilbert's left hind leg.

"Gilbert!" I cry, in the nick of time.

There is no need to go into the next five minutes. It will serve no purpose for me to repeat my weak explanation to the outraged Mrs. Garble that Gilbert, being still in the experimental stage, was merely about to test out a comparatively new idea. And that there was no personal malice or intended criticism involved.

Gilbert and I are alone again—and it is definitely time for me to take him out.

Gilbert *loves* to go out. Five, seven times a day he responds with mad joy to the rattle of his chain, dances with impatience as I attach his collar, and, in a series of chamois-like bounds, precipitates me to our apartment elevator, permitting me to touch the corridor with my feet only intermittently on the way.

If Gilbert is in luck, there will be another passenger in the elevator. This is a stout, very short gentleman with a red face who lives on the floor above us. He is generally on his way to some formal affair. There is something about his frock coats and silk hats which brings out Gilbert's warmest feelings of affection.

It takes Gilbert no time at all to place both his paws on the little man's carefully groomed shoulders. Gilbert's tongue then quickly and deftly leaves a long moist streak from chin to forehead, as Gilbert's body deposits large amounts of hair on the faultless apparel.

The little man's face now becomes even redder, because he does not understand dogs. I know he doesn't, because the very first time this occurred, I said to him reas-suringly, "It's all right, he is friendly."

To which he replied: "I'm not."

Since then all we say to each other is "Look out!"

Once we have left the elevator and passed through the lobby—a passage too swift for the average vision—Gilbert and I find ourselves outside. It is now that my problems begin and Gilbert's end. This is because we spend a lot of time standing by trees, lampposts, and pillars. It is not the fact that Gilbert is generally standing on one more leg than I am which makes my position more difficult than his. It is rather that I am far more conscious than he of the famous girls' finishing school on our block. Since its dismissal times seem to coincide with our airings, it bothers me to feel that there are hundreds of pretty young girls in the world who believe I spend my entire time standing by upright columns.

It is therefore frequently necessary for me to pretend

that I do not know Gilbert. This is difficult, because of the stout chain which connects us. There are various attitudes, however, which I assume:

1. That I happen to be out with a chain and a careless dog got caught in it.
2. That a dog happened to be out with a chain and I got caught in it.
3. That a chain happened to be out and the dog and I both got caught in it.

Between lampposts, Gilbert and I walk along with dignity. With as much dignity as possible, that is, considering that we are walking in the gutter.

Sometimes we pause in the gutter and turn around rapidly many times. Then one of us reads a newspaper, while the finishing school, which we are directly in front of, conducts a fire drill.

I could go on interminably. Maybe you think I have already. But anyway, we are agreed that my dog-handling methods are not ideal. Now let me give you some information which is really practical in case you plan to have a dog. Let us examine Gilbert's habits, his point of view, his psychology. I know all about them and it does me no good, but it may forewarn you abut your own dog.

I have observed many of Gilbert's moods. They are, I believe, fairly common to his race. Here are a few of them:

1. The *Hooray-Hooray-a-New-Day's-Dawning! Mood.*
   This manifests itself twice a day. Once at six in the morning, at which time Gilbert lands heavily on

my stomach, knocking both breath and sleep out of me. And a second time at a few moments past midnight, just after he has been bedded down, at which time he insists that I throw his rubber bone for him, or take him out with my coat over my pajamas. There must be some way to stop this.

2. The *Aren't-I-Supposed-to-Have-Any-Normal-Instincts-at-All? Mood*. This is caused simply by the fact that Gilbert is devoid of a sense of shame and I am not. It often results in our not speaking to each other and also in other people not speaking to me. There is no way to avoid this.

3. The *I-Was-Asleep-and-Some-Bad-Man-Must-Have-Come-in-and-Torn-That-Blue-Bedspread-to-Bits Attitude*. This is accompanied by a brazen, hypocritical simulation of overweening joy at my entrance and is unconvincing because of the large piece of blue cloth which Gilbert is unconsciously carrying on his dewlap. One method of avoiding this is always to leave your bed bare to the springs until retiring.

All right. Now that I have revealed my relationship to my dog in all its squalor, the curious may inquire why I have a dog at all. The curious may, but not the wise.

The answer, of course, is simple. In Gilbert I have found a being to whom I am superior in many ways, in spite of the fact that Phyllis insists that a lot more people stop to admire him than me on the street. Gilbert cannot drive a car. I can. Gilbert cannot wash dishes, pour drinks for people, run errands, or do dozens of other things around the house which Phyllis considers necessary. Above all, Gilbert is a living, breathing answer to her contention that I am the most inefficient form of life yet devised.

He is also the finest dog in town, even if he did tear up the very best parts of this piece.

This Dog's Life

Ann Patchett

It happened like this: after a walk in the park with a friend, I saw a young woman sitting in a car talking to a dog. Even from a distance, beneath the hard glass of the windshield, we could tell this was an exceptional animal. Never shy, I tapped on the young woman's door to ask her what kind of dog it was. We live in Nashville, where people do things like this and no one is frightened or surprised. The young woman told us the sad story: The dog, who on closer viewing was nothing but a mere slip of a puppy, had been dumped in a parking lot, rescued, and then passed among several well-intentioned young women, none of whom were allowed to have dogs in their apartments. Finally the dog had landed with the young woman in the car, who had been explaining to said dog that the day had come to look cute and find a permanent home.

The puppy was small and sleek and white. The sun came through her disproportionately large ears and showed them to be pink and translucent as a good Limoges cup held up to the light. We petted. She licked. We left the park with a dog.

I didn't think it would be this way. I thought when the time was right I would make a decision, consider breeds, look around. The truth is, I too was a woman who lived in an apartment that didn't accept dogs. But when fate knocks on the door, you'd better answer. "Let's call her Rose," my boyfriend said.

I was breathless, besotted. My puppy tucked her nose under my arm, and the hundred clever dog names I had dreamed up over a lifetime vanished. "Sure," I said. "Rose."

I was thirty-two years old that spring, and all I had ever wanted was a dog. While other girls grew up dreaming of homes and children, true love and financial security, I envisioned shepherds and terriers—fields of happy, bounding mutts. Part of my childhood was spent on a farm where I lived in a sea of pets: horses and chickens; a half a dozen sturdy, mouse-killing cats; rabbits; one pig; and many, many dogs—Rumble and Tumble and Sam and Lucy and especially Cuddles, who did justice to his name. Ever since that time I have believed that happiness and true adulthood would be mine at the moment of dog ownership. I would stop traveling so much. I would live someplace with a nice lawn. There would be plenty of money for vet bills.

At home, the puppy, Rose, played with balls, struggled with the stairs, and slept behind my knees while I watched in adoration. It's not that I was unhappy in what I now think of as "the dogless years," but I suspected things could be better. What I never could have imagined was how much better they would be. I had entered into my first relationship of mutual, unconditional love. I immediately found a much nicer apartment, one that allowed dogs for a ridiculously large, nonrefundable pet deposit. Since I work at home, Rose was able to spend her days in my lap, where she was most comfortable. We bonded in a way that some people looked upon as suspicious. I took Rose into stores like the rich ladies at Bergdorf's do. I took her to dinner parties. I took her to the Cape for vacation. As I have almost no ability to leave her alone, when I had to go someplace that foolishly did not allow dogs, I'd drive her across town and leave her with my grandmother. "Look at that," people said, looking at me and not Rose. "Look how badly she wants a baby."

A baby? I held up my dog for them to see, my bright, beautiful dog. "A dog," I said. "I've always wanted a dog." In truth, I have no memory of ever wanting a baby. I have never peered longingly into someone else's stroller. I have, on occasions too numerous to list, bent down on the sidewalk to rub the ears of strange dogs, to whisper to them about their limpid eyes.

"Maybe you don't even realize it," strangers said, friends said, my family said. "Clearly, you want a baby."

"Look at the way you're holding that dog," my grandmother said, "just like it's a baby."

People began to raise the issue with my boyfriend, insisting that he open his eyes to the pathetic scale of maternal want I was so clearly in. Being a very accommodating fellow, he took my hand. With his other hand he rubbed Rose's ears. He loves her as blindly as I do. Her favorite game is to be draped over the back of his neck like a fox-fur stole, two legs dangling on either shoulder. "Ann," he said, "if you want to have a baby . . ."

When did the mammals get confused? Who can't look at a baby and a puppy and see that there are some very marked differences? You can't leave babies at home alone with a chew toy when you go to the movies. Babies will not shimmy under the covers to sleep on your feet when you're cold. Babies, for all their many unarguable charms, will not run with you in the park, wait by the door for you to return, and, as far as I can tell, know absolutely nothing of unconditional love.

Being a childless woman of child-bearing age, I am a walking target for people's concerned analysis. No one looks at a single man with a Labrador retriever and says, "Will you look at the way he throws the tennis ball to that dog? Now, there's a guy who wants to have a son." A dog, after all, is man's best friend, a comrade, a buddy. But give a dog to a woman without children and people will say she is sublimating. If she says that she, in fact, doesn't want children, they will nod understandingly and say, "You just wait." For the record, I do not speak to my dog in baby talk, nor do I, when calling her, say, "Come to Mama."

"You were always my most normal friend," my friend Elizabeth told me, "until you got this dog."

While I think I would have enjoyed the company of many different dogs, I believe that the depth of my feeling for Rose in particular comes from the fact that she is, in matters of intelligence, loyalty, and affection, an extraordinary animal. In the evenings, I drive Rose across town to a large open field where people come together to let their dogs off their leashes and play. As she bounds through the grass with the

Great Danes and the Bernese mountain dogs, I believe that there was never a dog so popular and well adjusted as mine (and yet realize at the same time that this is the height of my own particular brand of insanity). The other dog owners want to talk about identifying her lineage, perhaps in hopes that one of her cousins might be located. It is not enough for Rose to be a good dog. She must be a particular breed of dog. She has been, depending on how one holds her in the light, a small Jack Russell, a large Chihuahua, a rat terrier, a fox terrier, and a corgi with legs. At present, she is a Portuguese Podengo, a dog that to the best of my knowledge was previously unknown in Tennessee. It is the picture she most closely resembles in our *International Encyclopedia of Dogs*. We now say things like "Where is the Podengo?" and "Has the Podengo been outside yet?" to give her a sense of heritage. In truth, she is a Parking-Lot Dog, dropped off in a snowstorm to meet her fate.

I watch the other dog owners in the park, married people and single people and people with children. The relationship each one has with his or her dog is very personal and distinct. But what I see again and again is that people are proud of their pets, proud of the way that they run, proud of how they nose around with the other dogs, proud that they are brave enough to go into the water or smart enough to stay out of it. People seem able to love their dogs with an unabashed acceptance that they rarely demonstrate with family or friends. The dogs do not disappoint them, or if they do, the owners manage to forget about it quickly. I want to learn to love like this, the way we love our dogs, with pride and enthusiasm and a complete amnesia for faults—in short, to love others the way our dogs love us.

When a dog devotes so much of herself to your happiness, it only stands to reason that you would want to make that dog happy in return. Things that would seem unreasonably extravagant for yourself are nothing less than a necessity for your dog. So my boyfriend and I hired a personal trainer for Rose. We had dreams of obedience, of *sit* and *stay* and *come*, maybe a few simple tricks. She didn't really seem big enough to drag the paper inside. I was nervous about finding the right trainer and called my friend Erica for moral support, but she was too busy going on interviews to get her four-year-old son into a top Manhattan preschool to be too sympathetic. The trainer we went with was the very embodiment of dog authority figures. After a few minutes of pleasant conversation in which Rose jumped on his shoulder and licked the top of his head, he laid out the beginnings of his plan.

Number one: The dog doesn't get on the furniture.

We blinked. We smiled nervously. "But she likes the furniture," we said. "We like her on the furniture."

He explained to us the basic principles of dog training. She has to learn to listen. She must learn parameters and the concept of *no*. He tied a piece of cotton rope to her collar and demonstrated how we were to yank her off the sofa cushion with a sharp tug. Our dog went flying through the air. She looked up at us from the floor, more bewildered than offended. "She doesn't sleep with you, does she?" the trainer asked.

"Sure," I said, reaching down to rub her neck reassuringly. She slept under the covers, her head on my pillow, her muzzle on my shoulder. "What's the point of having a twelve-pound dog if she doesn't sleep with you?"

He made a note in a folder. "You'll have to stop that."

I considered this for all of five seconds, "No," I said. "I'll do anything else, but the dog sleeps with me."

After some back-and-forth on this subject, he relented, making it clear that it was against his better judgment. For the duration of the ten-week program, either I sat on the floor with Rose or we stayed in bed. We celebrated graduation by letting her back up on the couch.

I went to see my friend Warren, who, handily, is also a psychologist, to ask him if he thought things had gotten out of hand. "Maybe I have an obsessive-compulsive disorder concerning my dog."

"You have to be doing something to be obsessive-compulsive," he said. "Are you washing her all the time? Or do you think about washing her all the time?"

I shook my head.

"It could be codependency, then. Animals are by nature very co-dependent."

I wasn't sure I liked this. Codependency felt too trendy. Warren's sixteen-year-old daughter, Kate, came in, and I asked her if she wanted to see the studio portraits I had taken of Rose for my Christmas cards. She studied the pictures from my wallet for a minute and then handed them back to me. "Gee," she said, "you really want to have a baby, don't you?"

I went home to my dog. I rubbed her pink stomach until we were both sleepy. We've had Rose a year now, and there has never been a cold and rainy night when I've resented having to take her outside. I have never wished I didn't have a dog, while she sniffed at each individual blade of grass, even as my hands were freezing up around the leash. I imagine there are people out there who got a dog when what they wanted was a baby, but I wonder if there aren't other people who had a baby when all they really needed was a dog.